BIG MATCH BINGO: FOOTBALL CLICHÉS – THE CLASSICS

Just cross off six heard in any match commentary and shout 'Bingo!'

A GAME OF TWO HALVES	A FAIR RESULT IN THE END	THE GAME NEEDS A GOAL	QUICK FEET	TO BE HONEST	GOOD FIRST TOUCH
A FUNNY OLD GAME	OUT OF ORDER	THIS WOULD BE THE PERFECT TIME TO SCORE	TO BE FAIR	BODIES IN THE BOX	DONE
I DIDN'T SEE THE INCIDENT...	WOULD HAVE SETTLED FOR THIS RESULT AT THE START...	NO SUCH THING AS AN EASY GAME THESE DAYS...	THE FULL SUPPORT OF THE CHAIRMAN AND THE BOARD	MADE A MEAL OF IT	
WE'LL TAKE EACH GAME AS IT COMES	DID EVERYTHING BUT SCORE	COULD HAVE GONE ANYWHERE	SET OUR STALL OUT	PURCHASE	
EARLY DOORS	LONG WAY TO GO	SORTING THE MEN FROM THE BOYS	STRAIGHT DOWN HIS THROAT	QUALITY BALL	

BIG MATCH BINGO: FOOTBALL CLICHÉS – PRE-MATCH

Just cross off six heard in any match commentary and shout **'Bingo!'**

MASSIVE TASK	DO NOT UNDERESTIMATE	MAKE NO MISTAKE ABOUT IT	NO EASY GAME	MIND GAMES
MUSTN'T CONCEDE	TOUGH OUTFIT	LEAGUE FORM COUNTS FOR NOTHING	FIRST GOAL IS VITAL	BIG PLAYERS
FINGERS CROSSED	NEED A PERFECT START	GUYS ARE UP FOR IT	ELECTRIFYING ATMOSPHERE	MUST GO FOR IT
LONG WAY TO GO	STANDING ON THE BRINK	ALL SET FOR THE BIG ONE	TARGET PLAYER	BITE YOUR NAILS TIME
TAKE THE GAME TO THEM	90 MINUTES AWAY FROM?	SOLID BACK FOUR	TEST OF CHARACTER	QUICK OUT OF THE BLOCKS
CAPABLE OF A GOAL OR TWO	MUSTN'T GET SUCKED IN	PRE-MATCH TENSION	VITAL	GLAMOUR TIE

Big Match Bingo

www.southbankpublishing.com

Other titles by the same author

Bullshit Bingo

Big Match Bingo

Graham Edmonds

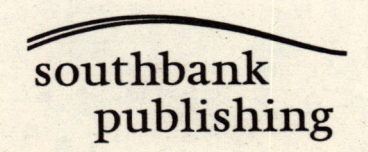

southbank
publishing

First published in 2006 by Southbank Publishing,
21 Great Ormond Street, London WC1N 3JB

www.southbankpublishing.com

© Graham Edmonds 2006

The right of Graham Edmonds to be identified as the author of this work has been asserted in accordance with the Copyright, Designs and Patents Act 1988.

All rights reserved. No part of this book may be reproduced, stored in or introduced into a retrieval system, or transmitted, in any form or by any means (electronic, mechanical, photocopying, recording or otherwise), without the written permission of the publishers.

Any person who does any unauthorised act in relation to this publication may be liable to criminal prosecution and civil claims for damages.

A CIP catalogue record for this book is available from the British Library.

ISBN 1 904915 16 7
EAN 978 1 904915 16 4

2 4 6 8 10 9 7 5 3 1

Typeset by Avocet Typeset, Chilton, Aylesbury, Bucks.
Printed and bound in Great Britain by Cox & Wyman, Reading.

*'I'm going to make a prediction —
it could go either way.'*

Attributed to Ron Atkinson

'So different from the scenes in 1872, at the Cup Final none of us can remember.'

John Motson

Chapters

Introduction		11
1.	Commentators and Pundits	13
2.	Big Ron	33
3.	What's in a Name?	39
4.	The Manager and the Chairman	47
5.	Are Any Managers Normal?	63
6.	They Broke the Mould... Brian Clough	71
7.	The Team, Teamwork and 'The Squad'	77
8.	It's All About the Game...	89
9.	Strachan	101
10.	Players	107
11.	Between the Sticks	117
12.	At the Back	125
13.	On the Charge	133
14.	Wit and Wisdom of the England Manager	143
15.	Romance of the Cup	149
16.	National Pride	155
17.	The B****** in the Black	169
18.	Who Said What?	175
19.	The Fans	183
Sources and Acknowledgements		187

Introduction

In the cliché-riddled world of football... managers take one game at a time, never see the crucial incidents and talk about getting the lads fired up. Players never take credit for their good performances; they do it for the team, they get involved, do a job and eventually hang up their boots. Commentators describe the big occasion while pundits discuss the talking points and generally sit on the fence.

Every match is full of commentary clichés; many are boring and old hat; some are entertaining, some just nuts. It all adds to the enjoyment of what is the most popular sport in the world.

In this book you'll find hundreds of clichés, quotes and, it has to be said, a fair bit of footie bullshit. Each is explained, analysed and generally abused.

To get you through the boring and most cliché-ridden matches we've invented the Big Match Bingo card. Just cross off the clichés as the match happens. Much more fun than the real thing...

1

Commentators and Pundits

'He's scored! There's no end to the stoppage of this drama...'

Alan Parry, commentator

Commentators and Pundits

Commentators tend to be journalists or enthusiastic supporters with the gift of the gab who have made it into radio. Pundits and summarisers are ex players who lend their expertise to the occasion. They should be celebrated, as without them this book wouldn't exist, and in fact there was a time when those running the game thought that providing a commentary to a match would ruin attendances.

Originally they were there just to describe what was going on, and when you listen to commentary from the Fifties and earlier it sounds a little like *Test Match Special* does today, but without the cake.

In the Sixties BBC's *Match of the Day* emerged as the leading football programme, joined eventually by similar programmes from the ITV regions. All had the same style; although pundits arrived in the Seventies on LWT's *Big Match* and although managers were often interviewed, it was a respectful affair and it was something of a novelty to hear the opinions of players and ex players.

Sadly some were (and some still are) pretty inarticulate, which led to much quoted lines such as **the boy done good** or clichés like **over the moon**. In the Eighties they got their own shows, such as Saint and Greavsie's *Football's a Funny Old Game* which, along with the still popular *Football Focus*, became the forerunners of shows popular today like *Soccer AM*.

There's no doubt that rather than hastening its demise, radio and television coverage has stimulated interest in the **game of football**. More recently, television coverage has been enhanced by the use of statistics and the ability to review a game on *Sky* by **pressing the red button** (although I know of no one who actually watches the player-cam).

We no longer have to rely solely on John Motson's or Martin Tyler's encyclopaedic knowledge — we can look up every statistic on the Internet and the Opta ratings system is a joy for most listings freaks and fantasy football players alike.

So then, nowadays a commentator can rely on reams of data, camera views from multiple angles, 'instant' replays and a whole team of technical experts to back them up and hype up the match, but that's not all.

In today's game a single commentator is not enough: they must have a sidekick, an ex player or manager who is there to provide the expert view, the insight of one who has been there; they are the co-commentators or, more recently, the summarisers. These people eventually graduate to the studio and onto punditry.

Commentators, summarisers, presenters and pundits have become as famous as the footballers themselves. Many have forthright views, are idiosyncratic and eccentric or downright boring, but without them life and football itself would be a little less interesting and what would we do for rumours and gossip?!

The Heroes of Commentary, Presenting and Punditry...

⚽ *Ron Atkinson*

No book like this would be complete without giving Big Ron a mention. You'll find 'Ronisms' throughout the book, although not many come better than: *'He actually looks a little twat, that Totti.'* His ability to come up with unique and daft commentary should be celebrated despite his recent annoying and stupid racist lapse; you'll find more of his exclamations and observations on page 35.

⚽ *Danny Baker*

The founder of *606*, the nation's favourite football feedback programme on Radio 5, chubby Baker has strong opinions about what being a fan is all about. This passion obviously affected his son, as in an interview Baker tells this story which happened while making a documentary about Paul Gascoigne. *'I'll never forget my boy Sonny, who'd have been three at the time – he didn't know who Paul Gascoigne was, and he came down later, at about eight in the morning, with his football; he wakes him up and asks if he wants to play football with him. So I'm lookin' out the window, and in the garden there's my three-year-old son saying, "I'll be England, you can be the dirty Germans", and I thought that's almost too good to be true, and Gazza's pattin' the ball to him, too polite to say, "Look, I just wanna get me head down".'*

⚽ *David Coleman*

Not best known as a football commentator but he has contributed to our cause by the invention by Private Eye of 'Colemanballs', a regular feature in which they list commentator's mistakes. Coleman was best known in football probably for his clipped *'one-nil'* as the first goal of the game was scored. By far his best quote has nothing to do with football, it was during the 1976 Olympics when he was commentating on the 800m final and as Cuban champion Alberto Juantorena accelerated down the back straight to win his gold medal Coleman said *'and the big Cuban opens his legs and shows his class…'*. Priceless.

⚽ *Helen Chamberlain*

One of the few women to break through into football as a presenter (the only other is Gabby Logan), a passionate Torquay United supporter, she fronts the cult Sky show *Soccer AM* with Tim Lovejoy. Chamberlain has a huge fan base and famously caused a bus crash when she modelled the Euro 2004 sports bra. When asked if she only got the job because she was a woman she said: *'I don't know and don't care.'*

⚽ *Garth Crooks OBE*

One of the best known black players of his day and with a

COMMENTATORS AND PUNDITS

successful career at Tottenham, Crooks was still a player when he started commentating. An all-round good egg and jolly nice chap, Crooks has the habit of asking (and replying to) the simplest of questions in the most complicated and convoluted way.

Adrian Chiles

A utility presenter for the BBC, moving effortlessly between radio, TV, football and business, Chiles is popular with fans mainly for his heartfelt support of West Bromwich Albion. He seems to live for their lack of success and can't hide it, especially when Birmingham or Villa performs better than his team.

Andy Gray

A successful centre forward playing for Scotland and many top clubs, Aston Villa and Everton among them, Gray has become Sky TV's top summariser and pundit. He has pioneered much of the technology that Sky seems obsessed with and that most of us rarely use. Earnest and forthright in his views with a distinctive Scottish brogue, he's not as mistake-prone as many of his colleagues but has the habit of calling all footballers '*son*' and when scoring is prone to suggesting that they '*take a bow*', while if it's a spectacular goal it's always '*out of the top drawer*'. Best attributed quote… '*It's one of the greatest goals ever, but I'm surprised that people are talking about it being the goal of the season.*'

BIG MATCH BINGO

⚽ *Alan Green*

Famously dour radio commentator with a distinctive Northern Irish accent, he's best known for getting his numbers muddled and announcing on air that Manchester Utd had won the championship when in fact it had gone to Blackburn. He has strong views on how the game should be played and especially hates it when players mimic the handing out of a red or yellow card. Excellent on hyperbole, he's particularly virulent when it comes to ugly football (*'shocking'*, *'should be banned'*, *'clubs penalised'* etc.) and showboating (*'disrespectful'*). Best attributed quote: *'This will be their 19th consecutive game without a win unless they can get an equaliser.'*

⚽ *Tony Gubba*

A veteran commentator who, while covering lots of sports for the BBC, is a football fan at heart. He, like many commentators, has a problem with numbers and percentages, with these quotes attributed to him: *'These two clubs had a monopoly of the domestic honours last season'*; *'Arsenal are quick to credit Bergkamp with laying on 75 per cent of their nine goals'*; *'Wigan Athletic are certain to be promoted barring a mathematical tragedy'*; and *'The ageless Teddy Sheringham, 37 now...'*

⚽ *Stuart Hall*

Ex presenter of *It's a Knockout* and owner of the maddest laugh on radio, Hall is best known for his use of flowery

COMMENTATORS AND PUNDITS

language for match descriptions, e.g. *'And here we are at the colosseum, with a match of titanic proportions about to take place. Will the gladitorial figurine of Owen add to his mighty goals tally?'* Sometimes though he is just unfathomable... *'Sheffield Wednesday the winners 2–0, leaving the Anfield crowd brainwashed.'*

⚽ Alan Hansen

Match of the Day pundit and ex Liverpool star best known for his comment on the young 1995 Manchester United side that *'you can't win anything with kids'*. They went on to win the Premiership that year. Hansen was a top defender in his day and his withering comments about teams that defend poorly have become a highlight of any *MOTD* programme... *'Naive defending'*, *'schoolboy error'*, *'shocking'*, *'massive'*, *'strength in depth'* and *'solid'* are all terms associated with him.

⚽ Jimmy Hill OBE

Beloved of impersonators in the Eighties, a pundit who had a successful career as a player with Fulham and with Coventry as manager, Hill is not as controversial as he once was, but nonetheless has got strong views about the game. He's been heavily involved with the game at the top level as chairman of the PFA, and is credited with coming up with the three points for a win system. He now hosts the *Sunday Supplement* show where he sits around with three invited journalists pontificating and generally talking bollocks about football over bacon and eggs. Not prone to errors, but apparently he did say of Beckham: *'He has two feet, which a lot of players don't have nowadays.'*

⚽ *Gary Lineker*

Another thoroughly nice chap (you know that because he never even got a booking as a professional player) who the BBC have turned into a front man for *Match of the Day*. He doesn't make many mistakes but he does have the habit of coming up with appalling puns none of which I feel should be repeated in this book.

⚽ *Gabby Logan*

Gabby is the pin-up girl in this mob. Bright, attractive and with the credibility that goes with being the daughter of footballer Terry Yorath, she's seen as a good choice to act as a presenter for the little bit of football coverage that ITV has these days. Married to a Scottish rugby player who thought he was actually dating Gaby Roslin!

⚽ *Des Lynam*

Old smoothy and housewives' favourite, Des has presented football shows on the BBC and ITV. *The Guardian* once referred to him as *'a mythical creature... half man, half moustache.'*

⚽ *Brian Moore*

Our commentary hero, sadly he died just a few hours

COMMENTATORS AND PUNDITS

before England thrashed Germany 5–1 and is remembered fondly as a true gent and someone who rarely made a mistake. His programme *The Big Match*, popular in its various guises throughout the Seventies and Eighties, pioneered the use of summarisers and pundits all drawn from ex professionals and successful managers. Without him this book wouldn't exist, so you'll get nothing but praise here.

⚽ *John Motson*

Motty, loathed and loved in equal measures, is today's senior commentator; he's been at it since the Seventies. A walking football encyclopaedia, he has a habit of coming out with obscure facts about players and their relatives during matches and raking up the past like no other; he's especially good at obscure references to England's World Cup win in 1966. He's sometimes spectacularly patronising, especially about players from countries where football isn't the major sport, but he has the knack of being constantly amazed at the game and perhaps this is what makes him so good. During his commentary he's always '*tempting fate*' or '*interrupting himself*' and he's been known to observe that '*the goals made such a difference to the way the game went*'.

⚽ *Jonathan Pearce*

Passionate Bristol City fan and the most excitable of commentators, Pearce has also become one of the most popular. King of the cliché, Pearce isn't prone to many errors although he is credited with: '*Vialli's absolutely certain that he knows one way or the other whether he'll score or not.'*

⚽ Saint and Greavsie

Ian St. John and Jimmy Greaves presented an irreverent football show in the Eighties which, despite the dodgy fashion (St. John's jumpers were usually multicoloured and always awful) and the crap jokes, was watched by millions. It paved the way for shows like Sky's *Soccer AM* and helped towards making celebrities out of players and pundits alike.

⚽ Chris Waddle

Outstanding player and owner of some of the dodgiest haircuts in football, Waddle spends time as a summariser and has a particular liking for the word **massive**. As a great player and England star he could be forgiven anything except his duet with Glenn Hoddle called *Diamond Lights*. At least he didn't take it seriously: Hoddle looked like he was really getting off on it, like it was a great song.

⚽ Kenneth Wolstenholme

Known as 'the voice of football' he was the Motson of his day, chiefly remembered for his '...*there are people on the pitch. They think it's all over; it is now...*' commentary in the 1966 World Cup Final. Amazingly, he commentated on twenty-three FA Cup Finals and five World Cups.

COMMENTATORS AND PUNDITS

Commentators' Tricks and Pundits Talking Bollocks...

The job of the commentator is to make the game as exciting as possible and each game is divided up into several phases...

Pre match

So firstly the media will **talk up** the game, and this is usually done by the presenters such as Sky's Richard Keys and those **back in the studio**. All matches are assumed to be big matches or **big occasions** and derby matches are always **massive**.

The next thing is to find an edge to the game, a talking point to make the match appear interesting to those fans that have no direct involvement or obvious interest in the game. For example...

- Historical rivalry between clubs and supporters. This can be national e.g. England v Germany, or local e.g. Liverpool v Everton, or even religious e.g. Celtic v Rangers.

- Reviewing previous crucial matches and incidents between the clubs. A common technique, especially for Premiership matches where Andy Gray takes us through old games and incidents which were always **crucial** or **vitally important**. Note that these incidents are never just 'vital'.

- Picking on certain players who are almost guaranteed to get involved in some controversial **incident** e.g. Robbie Savage,

Roy Keane, Wayne Rooney. Usually described as **handbags** if the incident is fairly tame or a **mass brawl** if it really gets out of hand, but whatever happens there will always be the mention of **raised hands**.

- Edited highlights from pre match (or old) interviews geared to make something appear controversial e.g. interviewing a manager before the match and asking open questions like… *'How do feel about your opposition?'* or, for example, asking Sir Alex Ferguson what his thoughts are on Arsene Wenger.

- The weather or **playing conditions**. If it's hot then there will be concern that the players **take on enough fluids**, if it's cold then the **pitch will be called into question** which also happens if it's been raining too hard. A greasy surface is ideal for exciting football apparently, although no one mentions exactly what type of grease is used.

- The pitch, or more usually the **state of the pitch** which can be described as anything from a ploughed field to a bowling green; when commentators attempt to get technical they call it **the playing surface**. In cup matches between a **big club** and a **minnow** it can be a **great leveller**, while at some grounds the pitch is described as **hallowed turf**. For derby matches, if the commentator really wants to stir things up he will only have to mention the magic words **ground share** to get the required over-the-top reaction.

- **Tempting fate** is common especially during England matches, when the commentator or summariser will always say how well England is playing just moments before the

COMMENTATORS AND PUNDITS

opposition scores. Having said that most commentators are loath to make predictions of any sort, pundits usually **sit on the fence** when it comes to predicting results.

⚽ Along with **class**, commentators talk a lot about **character**. It's a **test of character** for a team when they **go behind** to an **early goal** or lose a key player who is the victim of a **harsh decision**. Players have to show character when playing in these conditions and, in particular, when they have suffered a tragedy outside of football, especially one that **puts things into perspective**.

Everything is geared to make the dullest matches seem more exciting than they really are and, as a general rule, the more hype before the match the worse the game is.

Half-time

Talking points and incidents from the first half are discussed, lots of surmising about what is going on in the dressing rooms, more predictions, and more attempts to build tension.

Extensive replays are used on Sky where everything seems more definitive e.g. **without a shadow of a doubt**, and with their never-ending use of technology they obsess about eking out the truth behind every **incident** and **talking point**.

Other typical half-time traits or first half commentary classics said by pundits (and commentators) are…

BIG MATCH BINGO

- **He's got to be careful** – about any player who gets a yellow card in the early stages in the game.

- **It's gone in!** – said in great surprise when someone scores from a shot that was meant to be a cross or when it's an own goal.

- **One-nil** – said in a clipped tone as though it was obvious to everyone that it was only a matter of time before the attacking team scored, or as though their prediction was vindicated.

- Both pundits and commentators mystify viewers by talking about **putting the ball into the channels**. They do this a lot, especially at half-time reviews, and those of us without knowledge or who are just too old to learn new tricks assume they mean down the wing.

- Chances of a goal are viewed as **gilt-edged** or **gift-wrapped** if it's a near miss, or **put into row Z** if the striker has missed wildly.

- Repeating the same point over and over prefacing it with **I know I keep saying it but…** or using the unfathomable **at the risk of repeating myself**.

- Using the word **irony** or **isn't it ironic that** when it's really just a coincidence. Motson excelled himself during England's 5–1 win over Germany: when one of the goals was scored he delighted in pointing out how ironic it was that the clock showed 66 minutes… it was just a coincidence!!!

COMMENTATORS AND PUNDITS

- When both sides are **committed to attack** it's described as **end-to-end** stuff.
- Whenever something is in the balance it's always **touch and go** or **it could go either way**, and whatever happens the **first goal is vital** as is drawing **first blood**.

- Whenever a commentator or pundit has a controversial pet theory, instead of plugging it as their own idea they will say **he's many people's idea of…** or mention something that is **well documented**, thereby putting over the idea without having to take responsibility for it.

Post match

After the final whistle has gone it's the time for interviews and attempts by the media to make players and managers say something controversial. It's time to take the piss out of those pundits who got the score completely wrong, and try and build up the next game. For fans it's time to bemoan their bad luck if their team has lost or to paint the town red if they have won.

For pundits it's more clichés…

- Being wise after the event e.g. **as I said earlier Brian** or **as I predicted**. Mind you it is quite impressive when they actually get it right.

- **A great advert for the game** – usually said when a match is actually better and more exciting than expected. Matches like that are **good for the game of football**.

BIG MATCH BINGO

- **They'll be dancing in the streets of** (insert some dump of a town) **tonight** when the team from the dump has won…

- A commentator will say **honours even** if they think a draw is a **fair result**.

- Whenever a player or team does something good, they will be **answering their critics**.

- When something unusual happens they will say something along the lines of **you can't legislate for that**. In fact, they are unable to say the word 'can't', it will be 'cannot' but said as though it's two words i.e. **you can not legislate for that**…

- Commentators, in particular, have an obsession with class. It's either the **gulf in class** between the two teams or the difference in class between players, or that they should be allowed to **show their class**. Apparently **class always tells in the end** and some players such as Ryan Giggs (but not those like Rooney) are always **classy** while losing teams are nearly always **outclassed**.

- Excess use of the word 'completely' as in **completely over the top** with variations such as 'totally' as in **totally out of order** or 'comprehensively' as in **comprehensively beaten** is a feature of *Match of the Day*, whose pundits are sometimes painfully unbiased, with the possible exception of Alan Hansen.

Love them or hate them we can't be without them and this book is a testament to the commentator, the pundit and the vocabulary they have created.

Big Match Bingo – Commentators and Pundits' Standard Clichés

You cannot legislate for that	He's got to be careful	They'll be dancing in the streets of…	Gilt-edged	I don't want to tempt fate but…	Talking point
Class	The game of football	At the risk of repeating myself	Greasy surface	Call into question	Big club
Big occasion	Crucial	Massive	Leveller (pitch or weather)	Channels	Vitally important
A great advert for the game	Answering his/their critics	End-to-end stuff	Touch and go	Saying 'can not' instead of 'can't'	Irony
Weathered the storm	Sorting the men from the boys	Out of order	Strength in depth	Quality ball	Long way to go
State of the pitch	I know I keep saying this but…	Handbags	Gift-wrapped	As I said earlier…	Raised hands

Just cross off six heard in any match commentary and shout 'Bingo!'

2

Big Ron

'Look! It's Big Ron – and what's he up to? Why, he's clumsily trampling all over the English language of course.'

The Guardian

Ronglish

Ron Atkinson was always one of the most high profile managers (helped by a dodgy but distinctive haircut, a great and well-topped-up tan and lots of jewellery) then, despite being one of the first managers to introduce ethnic players into the game, he made a stupid racist remark on live TV and rightly lost his job over it.

For those who think of Atkinson in a negative light after that, it should be pointed out, for balance, that during the late Seventies when racism in football was arguably at its height, Big Ron (then at West Brom) fielded three black players (Brendon Batson, Laurie Cunningham and Cyrille Regis) in his team. At the time this was seen as a real move forwards and a positive step which paved the way and allowed more black players into the game.

For this generation he's known less for success as a player or manager, it's as a pundit that he has come to prominence with a whole host of 'Ronisms' that seem to have worked their way into the language of football.

Ron's terms as adopted by other commentators...

☻ **Amusement arcade** – skilful but ineffective play.

- ⚽ **Back stick** – the far post.

- ⚽ **Blinder** – a great performance.

- ⚽ **Early doors** – early part of a game.

- ⚽ **Have a dig** – shoot.

- ⚽ **Hollywood ball** – an overambitious pass.

- ⚽ **Little eyebrows** – an intentional glancing header.

- ⚽ **Locker** – as in **what's he got left in his locker?**

- ⚽ **Lollipop** – a trick played by one footballer on another as in **he's lollipopped 'im.**

- ⚽ **Reducer** – a heavy challenge.

- ⚽ **Spotter's badge** – awarded to any player playing a great pass.

- ⚽ **Tell you what John…**

Here's a none too comprehensive list of his attributed commentarial highlights…

- ⚽ *'…and Schmeichel extends and grows even bigger than he is.'*

- ⚽ *'He's gone up and given the centre half a short back and sides there. Look at the replay, there's dead hair all over the six yard box.'*

- *'I think that was a moment of cool panic there.'*

- *'If Glenn Hoddle said one word to his team at half-time, it was concentration and focus.'*

- *'I've just seen Kevin Keegan shake hands with Jurgen Klinsmann, it's a wonder Klinsmann hasn't fallen down.'* Referring to the German striker's diving abilities.

- *'If he thinks he's going to get away with that he's been watching cartoons.'*

- *'They must go for it now as they have nothing to lose but the match.'*

- *'They've come out at half-time and gone bang.'*

- *'They've picked their heads up off the ground, and they now have a lot to carry on their shoulders.'*

- *'Well, Clive, it's all about the two M's — movement and positioning.'*

- *'You can't legislate for skill like that. He's done a right Pan's People on John O'Shea there.'*

- *'He dribbles a lot and the opposition don't like it — you can see it all over their faces.'*

- *'That boy throws a ball further than I go on holiday.'* On long throw specialist Dave Challinor of Tranmere Rovers.

BIG MATCH BINGO

The last word…

⚽ When managing one of his many clubs Ron was standing on the touchline as his striker got involved in a collision. The trainer ran onto the pitch to see the player and on reporting back said that the lad was concussed and didn't know what his name was. Ron helpfully suggested: *'Tell him he's Pele and send him back on.'*

3

What's in a Name?

'Julian Dicks is everywhere. It's like they've got eleven Dicks on the field.'

Radio commentary attributed to several stations.

Big Match Bingo's Guide to Unfortunate Names

Commentators have to liven up their patter by building the image of players and sometimes managers (e.g. calling Mourinho **The Special One**).

Some players are so good and so well known that they become known by one name – Pele, Maradona, Gazza and so on – while some have a physical attribute that lends itself well to a nickname. One of the earliest on record is Fatty Foulkes, a twenty-stone goalkeeper who played for Sheffield United in the 1890s.

The nickname

- As with most places of work, the workers like to give each other nicknames. First off there are those that derive from the players name, such as **One Size** for Crystal Palace defender Fitz Hall or **The Goat** for Shaun Goater. Then there's the ones you have to think about such as Marc **Freezer** Goodfellow, or the ones you don't like John **Tumble** Dreyer. One of the best belongs to Kiki Musampa, who has the nickname **Chris**.

- Some names come from the media. John Barnes was sometimes known as **Digger** due to the popularity of

Dallas, while striker Nathan Ellington gets to be called the **Duke**. Barnes was also called **Tarmac** because he was the new Heighway (for those of you who don't remember black and white telly, Steve Heighway was a Liverpool star of the Seventies).

- Then there are those nicknames that arise from the player's demeanour, such as **Psycho** (Stuart Pearce) or **Chopper** (Seventies Chelsea hero Ron Harris). Some get something aggressive such as **Razor** Ruddock or **The Guv'nor** (Paul Ince), or ones that suggest they are just a little bit mad, such as **Crazy Horse** (Emlyn Hughes). Mark Hughes was called **Sparky**, not because of his on-pitch exploits, but because he was such a quiet lad.

- The media are pretty good at applying nicknames, especially ones that sum up the player, such as **The Kaiser** for Franz Beckenbauer or, one that is of it's time, **The Galloping Major** for Hungarian star Ferenc Puskas. Some are just plain daft, such as Roberto Baggio's the **Divine Ponytail**, but it's entertaining nonetheless, while drug user and sacked ex Chelsea player Adrian Mutu was called **Puff Daddy** by his Chelsea teammates.

- It has to be said though that foreign players do get the best nicknames. For example, Emilio Butragueno gets to be called **The Vulture**, Hristo Stoichkov **The Pitbull**, Roy Makaay **The Phantom**, the exception being Romario, who gets to be called **Shorty**.

- There's even regional variations throughout the world;

WHAT'S IN A NAME?

African teams like animals such as **Lions** or **Eagles**, while continental Europeans tend to go for the romantic (Marco Van Basten **The Swan from Utrecht**) or the obvious (Claudio Pizarro, **Pizza**). In South America they go for names like the **Matador** (Mario Kempes), anything red blooded and masculine will do.

- Anyone who looks young for their years is said to be **baby-faced**; it applied particularly to Manchester United striker Ole Gunnar Solskjaer, but also players like Michael Owen. *The Guardian*, though, referred to Wayne Rooney as an **assassin-faced baby**.

Team nicknames

- Any injury-prone player gets to be called **Sick Note**, most famously associated with Darren Anderton.

- Anyone with a small penis is called **inchy**, anyone with a large one it's **donkey**. Although, Tony Adams did get this label mainly because of his habit of **hoofing** the ball anywhere up field; this was usually met with the crowd shouting 'Eeyore!'

- Barry was also quite bald and we all know bald players just get called **slaphead**.

- Anyone who is skilful tends to get called **Magic**, especially if their name is Johnstone or Johnson.

- Anyone whose name starts Mc or Mac is usually called **Macca**, especially if they come from anywhere near Liverpool.

Given by the fans

Some fan nicknames get very obscure and cruel, but here's a few that we have garnered from our travels...

- Kieron Richardson at Manchester United is known as **The White Towel** because when he comes on **it's like they're giving up.**

- Ineffective winger Jesper Gronkjaer was nicknamed Dracula because he was afraid of crosses.

- After keeper Andy Goram was diagnosed as having schizophrenia, he would be greeted with the chant **there's only two Andy Gorams...**

- Any overweight players take the field to the song **who ate all the pies** and usually just get called **pies**, as in Sunderland's Paul Butler. The same team also had a chubby goalie named Barry **Flying Pig** Siddall. Number one pie-eater though was Mick Quinn, who the Coventry fans gave the name **Sumo**.

- Denis Bergkamp was nicknamed the **non-flying Dutchman** because of his fear of air travel.

WHAT'S IN A NAME?

- Probably the best fan-given nickname goes to reluctant striker Savo Milosevic, who got labelled **Misalotevic**.

Getting clever (or lazy)

- Most commonly there's the habit of putting an 'o' or 'y' on the end of a name, so **Keano** or **Barnesy** for example, or general name shortening, especially for foreign players.

- Putting 'zza' on the end of names (e.g. **Gazza**) seems to have drawn to an end, but commentators like to be clever and use the suffix '-esque' whenever they get the chance. So if a player makes a surging run through a defence it's called **Gazzaesque**, or if they attempt to chip the keeper it's called **Hoddlesque**, but if it all goes wrong and they make a mess of it it's usually just called a **Drogba** (actually I made that one up).

You have to feel sorry for them

We can only wish that Turkmenistani politician Mustapha Kunt has a son of the same name who becomes a Premiership star, or that Ginger Minge of the Electra High School in Texas goes on to have a football crazy son, but spare a thought though for those foreign players who, on hearing that they would soon be playing in England, would be excited at the prospect of being announced to the expectant crowd.

- People like Swedish international Dick Last or Dutch

defender Johan de Kock, Danny Shittu, Nwankwo Kanu and the Dutch star Brian Pinas.

⚽ Others that (sadly) never made it to our shores are Milan Fukal, a Czech defender, porn star soundalike Johnny Moustache, German players Holger Ballwanz and Stefan Kuntz, and a Portuguese goalkeeper by the name of Quim.

⚽ Even British players can't avoid the stigma of a name that sounds slightly rude; take Paul Dickov or Julian Dicks for example. No doubt Marcus and Darren Bent, Danny Hercock and David Sheepshanks come in for plenty of stick too; in fact anyone with 'bottom' or 'cock' in their name gets the treatment. For managers Arthur Cox and Alan Dicks it must have been fun for them and those fans that wanted them 'out'.

⚽ Top of the tree in the names league has to go to Argelico Fuks (apparently known as Argel) and the Eurosport editor who allegedly printed the headline *'Argel Fuks off to Benfica'*.

Commentators Nightmare Utd

1. Quim

2. Dicks   4. Fukal   5. Moustache   3. de Koch

6. Ballwanz   7. Kuntz   8. Shittu   11. Pinas

10. Bent   9. Dickov

Subs – Fuks, Hercock, Sheepshanks

Manager – A Cox

4

The Manager and the Chairman

'If a chairman sacks the manager he initially appointed, he should go as well.'

Brian Clough on the fact that too many managers lose their jobs too soon.

'At last England have appointed a manager who speaks English better than the players.'

Clough on the appointment of Sven-Goran Eriksson.

Chairmen, Owners and the Club

'The ideal board of directors should comprise three men – two dead and one dying.'

Tommy Docherty, famous serial manager

Type 'football club chairmen' into Google and up pops a litany of failures, boardroom bust ups and the missives of new chairmen as they take over previously mismanaged (in their opinion) clubs.

It's a well-known truth that chairmen come and go, but fans stay at a club for life. It seems that most of those fans don't trust their shareholders and especially those at the top. In the quest for instant success, some chairmen (and their board) have a reputation for sacking managers without really giving them a chance, although that's often got as much to do with the impatience of the fans as the board… take Newcastle United for example.

Some chairmen are on an ego trip, but they are often hard-working benefactors who feel the urge to 'put something back into the community' and live out their footballing fantasies through club ownership.

BIG MATCH BINGO

> *'Roman Abramovich has parked his Russian tanks on our lawn and is firing £50 notes at us.'*
>
> **David Dein, Arsenal Vice Chairman**

The clubs themselves fall into several categories…

- **Ambition** – a club **with ambition** is usually a small club who, with the help of a well-moneyed benefactor, morphs into a bigger club with higher goals than before. This is a matter of degree though, as before being bought by Roman Abramovich Chelsea would have only dreamt of Champion's League involvement and they're now busy turning themselves into one of the game's giants.

- **Big Club** – before 'Abramovich's millions' Chelsea would not have been classed as a Big Club just because they had won comparatively little. That moniker was reserved for the likes of Manchester United, Arsenal and Liverpool and 'north of the border' Rangers and Celtic. Clubs who have had **illustrious histories** or with exceptional support are sometimes labelled in this way, usually Spurs, Leeds United, Everton, Villa, Man City and Newcastle.

- **Fashionable** – usually applied to London or big city clubs who attract players because of the local social scene rather than the money they pay. So Spurs are fashionable and Scunthorpe isn't. Commentators sometimes use the word **glamour** instead of fashionable, which basically means they're within walking distance of a decent night club or casino.

THE MANAGER AND THE CHAIRMAN

- **Giant** – only applied to clubs such as Barcelona, Real Madrid, Manchester United etc., something the others aspire to be e.g. Chelsea.

- **In Transition** – this happens when a previously successful club loses its way, usually due to former great managers and players retiring or leaving. The hope is that **success is just round the corner** and the new management and players can recapture **past glories**.

- **Minnow** – a local or lower league team. This term is usually reserved for times when playing a bigger club in the cup competitions. Whenever a minnow wins anything, it's called a **fairy tale.**

- **Overachiever** – a club that, through shrewd management (or who have the luck to get hold of a group of exceptional players), achieves a degree of success that is not necessarily expected of them, so currently Bolton, Wigan and Charlton.

- **Sleeping Giant** – usually a **Big Club** either gone into decline or a club in a permanent state of underachievement like Newcastle United (virtually all clubs are sleeping giants then).

- **Unfashionable** – clubs that usually have never won anything and probably never will, usually from a small town. It applies up to the point the club gets a chairman who has pots of money, and then it is amazing how quickly they become **fashionable** or **a club with ambition.**

BIG MATCH BINGO

History plays an important part in any club's culture – it seems that in the mind of the commentator and for the club it's either on their side or it isn't. Clubs often take on the personal qualities of the chairman and vice versa, the Wimbledon team of the Nineties being a case in point, but most clubs have a strong tradition and their teams have a style of playing that goes back decades, and in interviews chairmen in particular have a habit of saying things like '*and that's what this club is all about…*'.

- The best chairmen **bring glory** to the club using their money to win championships (Blackburn and Jack Walker) though most often it's a case of guaranteeing survival, and they are beloved of the fans and the media alike.

- With the possible exception of Freddy Shepherd and Doug Hall of Newcastle*, it's a case of woe betide those chairmen and directors who denigrate their fans or the club they own. The worst crime is to **treat it like a business** and **expect to make a profit**, and talking about the **bottom line** is a big no-no. Fans expect the club owners to give their money freely to the cause and (with shades of the Roman Empire) will worship them for it, especially if **success comes their way**.

---

* In a classic tabloid sting, while allegedly on a visit to a Spanish brothel Shepherd and Hall likened their best player, Alan Shearer, to Mary Poppins, boasted of the huge mark-up they made on the sale of club shirts and to top it all said that Newcastle women were all 'dogs'. Shepherd seemed to ignore the point made by one of the fans that his two daughters were born in Newcastle.

THE MANAGER AND THE CHAIRMAN

- A club is said to be **in turmoil** when their finances go awry, and **calling in the administrators** is considered the worst situation as it could lead to the club **ceasing to exist**. Any decisions announced are made **in the best interests of the club** to **secure its future** and ensure football is played there **for many years to come**. This is when fans hear what they have been dreading, with talk of **ground sharing** or moving to a **new stadium** (usually on a green-field site, miles from the town) or their worst nightmare, the merging with another club to **ensure survival**.

- The main role of the chairman then is to act as provider, **to make funds available**, and it's OK for them to go on an ego trip providing the club is successful. The chairman has one other duty and that is to find and appoint the manager. A new manager is to be treasured, brought in when the board think it's **time for a change, a fresh start** or after **a poor run of results**. They are given the **full backing of the board** and told to go out and get results. The manager then is the subject of the next section.

The Manager, the Gaffer, the Guv'nor and the Boss

Either loved or hated, there seems no in between for football managers (or 'the Gaffer' as players would have it) and this has driven them to behave in certain ways, especially those with high media profiles. There is a set of rules that they all seem to follow, a set of sayings, axioms and behaviours which they all learn.

Big Match Bingo's guide to managers' behaviours

- Always **take each game as it comes** or a **game at a time** because being seen to plan for anything more than that is seen as a bit premature or even tempting fate. This assumes that behind-the-scenes planning is being done for more than one game in advance, but managers cannot be seen to do anything other than concentrate on the next match (usually 100 per cent).

- **I didn't see it myself...** They never see the controversial incident of the match, especially when their player is involved. This could lead to more involvement in the media and more unnecessary controversy. The leading exponent of this non-observational ability is Arsene Wenger of Arsenal.

- For those managers that chose to see the incident, the referee is always in the wrong when the decision goes against their team, unless they have won the match. Then they can afford to be magnanimous and agree that it was a penalty or their player should have been sent off. The referee is always right when the decision is in their favour.

- The referee always has a **difficult job**. This is always said before the word 'but', the manager then goes on to point out the referee's shortcomings. Some never comment on referees at all, summed up in the words of Ron Atkinson: *'I never comment on referees and I'm not going to break the habit of a lifetime for that prat.'*

THE MANAGER AND THE CHAIRMAN

⚽ Manager love using mixed metaphors and like pundits and players manage to combine poor grammar with the inability to complete words or sometimes understand what they mean. Take these examples...

'If you can't stand the heat in the dressing room, get out of the kitchen.' Terry Venables

'The tide is very much in our court now.' Kevin Keegan

'If we played like this every week, we wouldn't be so inconsistent.' Attributed to both Bryan Robson and Sir Alex Ferguson.

'Samassi Abou don't speak the English too good.' Harry Redknapp

Nowadays the most common mistakes by those being interviewed are grammatical, for example substituting 'themselves' with 'theirselves' or in co-commentary the common **he's come for the ball**. Clipping the end of words that end in 'ly' is still around; **he done fantastic** is the classic, not as common as it used to be (sadly) although Birmingham manager Steve Bruce manages to keep it going.

> *'Francis could not, in my opinion, spot a great footballer if the bloke's name had four letters in it, starting with P and ending in an E.'*
>
> **Former player Alan Hudson on Trevor Francis's managerial skills.**

BIG MATCH BINGO

- They all seem to have a **love-hate** relationship with the media, simultaneously hating the coverage they get when things go bad while lapping up the praise when things are going well. Some managers actively seek out and use the media to get their own agenda messages to their players, fans or even their chairmen (especially as their contract is coming up for renewal), while others shy away and hate giving even the shortest interview. Being media savvy is a must these days, Sven Goran-Eriksson (and his agent's) inability to spot a fake sheikh is probably a little on the extreme side but even the managers of the lowliest clubs must beware of the open question like: 'how did you feel about the game?'

- The ability to have a good sulk is one of the more recent trends in football management, a good example being Sir Alex Ferguson's long running 'I'm not talking to the BBC 'cause they were rude about me' bit of petulance, although this may now have developed into something of a wind-up.

- Conversely, it's essential that the manager has the ability to give a good bollocking (commentary speak is **a tough talking to**) to players and team alike. Sir Alex's 'hairdryer treatment' is legendary and for those players who had it up and close something they'll never forget, even though they may not have understood a word of it. Brian Clough was known as an expert in the quick witted and precise skewering of his intended victim, a process sometimes called **kebabbing**. When a good telling-off is obviously on the cards commentators always say **I'd like to be a fly on**

THE MANAGER AND THE CHAIRMAN

the wall in that dressing room or **the plates will be flying** or something about broken crockery.

⚽ Whether it is for personal gain, buying players or club finances, the manager must have a good head for money. Buying players comes with its own set of clichés; managers and clubs are said to be **plotting a swoop** or **brandishing their chequebook**, making a **high profile acquisition**, looking for the **right player**, the money being **available or there ready to be spent** when the time comes or the **right player comes along**, as though there is some sort of player factory.

⚽ At this point the term **bung** raises its ugly head. Corruption is said to be common place in transfer dealings and agents are often classed as **scum** when really they are trying to get the best deal for their clients, the players. It's just that sometimes they get a little over enthusiastic… **Honest Guv, gospel, cross me heart… never seen that fat brown envelope before…**

⚽ The ability to turn a negative into a positive is a key part of the manager's skill set. A poor game is turned into **a bad day at the office** which takes the heat off the players, **lessons are learned** and emphasis is taken away from the defeat by talking about the importance of the next match. Occasionally **there's nowhere to hide** and this is where the manager apologises to the fans and **takes it on the chin**.

⚽ Negotiation skills are an important ability, especially when the contract talks start. Usually, if the existing manager is wanted, these will take place some 18 months ahead of the end of the **current agreement**. The manager will talk of **honouring his contract** (which he probably won't) and **how much the club** (and the fans) **mean to him**. If he wants to stay then it's all very amicable. But if he wants to go then the situation will become **difficult** at first, then as **talks break down** it will **become impossible** and he'll be left with **no choice but to go**, usually taking a big pay-off too.

The knowledge of players' psychology, the ability to manipulate egos, build confidence and generally motivate are all essential management skills, but what other little sayings and clichés do you hear? Here's a list...

- **A few more grey hairs** – this is usually said when there's been a close victory or an achievement has been made against the odds. Of course it depends on the manager having grey hairs in the first place, Mark Hughes being the outstanding candidate. Baldies and those with strange haircuts (Sven) need not bother.

- Afford the luxury or more often **can't afford the luxury**, usually of an underperforming player or superstar whose value to the team has lessened.

- **All credit to** – the lads (who worked their socks off), the referee (who spotted the incident), the opposition (who gave them a good game but lost) and the chairman (who gave them 110 per cent support).

- **Backing of the board** or getting the chairman's full

THE MANAGER AND THE CHAIRMAN

support is the precursor for the sack, it's the **writing on the wall** and everyone knows it's all over when the manager gets the dreaded **vote of confidence**.

✪ **Bow out** – whenever a manager (or a player for that matter) leaves the game or the job in a relatively positive way they **bow out**, dunno why, they just do.

✪ **Caretaking capacity** – a sort of football limbo taken on by assistant managers, youth team coaches or managerial old lags who take **temporary charge of team affairs** after the manager has been sacked.

✪ **Caught a cold on that one** – said after taking a drubbing.

✪ **Consistency** is a key part of Chelsea's success and their ability to **grind out results, week in week out** is **the mark of a great team**, and especially **when playing badly they still get results**.

✪ **Gambles** usually come at a point in the match when the manager must make changes to either get a result or save the match, sometimes though he must **gamble on a player's fitness** or take a gamble tactically, **reverting to a 4–4–2** from a 3–5–1–1 formation for example. Either way the gamble can have career-changing results.

✪ For some, the **dressing room** is an almost mythical place where the manager can show his true worth, **inspiring the troops**, dispensing bollockings to underperforming players, praising those worthy few who contribute more than usual and **losing the plot** when it all goes tits up. The worst thing a manager can do is **lose the dressing room**, meaning that his players no longer pay attention to his demands – this usually spells the beginning of the end and unless he makes some **worthwhile additions to the squad** he'll be out on his ear. Players meanwhile are either **real characters** in the dressing room or classed as **quiet**; there seems to be no in-between and it's a key management skill to get the **right balance** between the two.

- **Over the moon** – classic manager speak for those times when all plans come to fruition and they get a good result. It's rarely used these days and has been replaced by more mundane terms as managers have been media trained and are aware of talking in clichés, however luckily we still have the likes of Steve Bruce, Iain Dowie and Ian Holloway to **keep the faith**.

- Potentially disastrous, **looking on helplessly from the sidelines** comes into use when all the gambles have been taken and the poor sap of a manager has to stand there while his team take a drubbing. It can be energy sapping; you only have to look at the expression on the faces of the likes of Mick McCarthy and Graeme Souness in the 2005/6 season to see that. The **man in charge** can only attempt to **put on a brave face** and talk about **lessons learned, putting the defeat behind them** and **looking forward to the next match**. Those managers in real trouble **vow to fight on** and tell the media that they are **not a quitter** and that they are **determined to see it through**.

THE MANAGER AND THE CHAIRMAN

⚽ The power of **positive thinking** is probably epitomised by the likes of Iain Dowie at Crystal Palace; it seems to shield the team from the effects of defeat and the general malaise that can take over. Compare and contrast Mick McCarthy's body language in the 2004/5 season while winning the Championship in style with Sunderland, to that of the 2005/6 season when the same team languished adrift at the bottom of the Premiership. For most managers though it's a case of thinking 'positive thinking – my arse!' then rolling their sleeves up and getting on with the **pure hard graft** which, as we all know, always gets results.

⚽ Some managers take the power of positive thinking to the extreme and even when **facing the inevitable** will not concede defeat until it is mathematically impossible to say otherwise. To be seen to admit defeat is, in the eyes of the fans, tantamount to treason, so managers are rightly very careful.

Players who do well are described as **real characters**, they **stand up to be counted** and **make their mark on the game**, even **taking it by the scruff of its neck**. However **it's not about individuals**, it's about the team, but then someone always needs **to stand up and be counted**.

5

Are Any Managers Normal?

'My manager wants me to dress like a nun and I want to dress like a teenager.'

**Anna Kournikova
(nothing to do with football but hey…)**

The Manager's Lot is not a Happy One...

When you look back on the game's successful managers it's almost impossible to find a normal bloke amongst them; the only possible exception is Alan Curbishley who you can imagine helping his wife with the shopping, but most seem completely nuts or at the very least mildly eccentric. Apart from the earnest **young guns** (Chris Coleman, Iain Dowie, Paul Jewell) and the hardworking journeymen (namely most managers from the lower divisions) managers appear to fall into several key characters traits...

- The **hard men** with their leathery skins, passion and an uncompromising view of the game, capable of great acts of kindness and sympathy alongside their tough, no-nonsense attitude.

    Bill Shankly – worshipped still at Liverpool as the man who started their great run of success in the Seventies and onwards. After beating Everton in the cup he said: *'Sickness would not have kept me away from this one. If I'd been dead, I would have had them bring the casket to the ground, prop it up in the stands and cut a hole in the lid.'*

    Sir Alex Ferguson – a bit of a control freak, much respected and the scourge of match officials everywhere. He plays the psychological game better than any other manager, a master at stating the *'bleeding obvious'*, his temper sometimes gets the better of him. For example, when being questioned by journalists about bad buy Juan Sebastian Veron he said: *'I'm not f**king talking to you. He's a f**king great player and yous all f**king idiots.'* As Gary Lineker once said: *'A strange bloke, irritated by everyone, I think.'*

- **Ex great players** don't always make the best managers but many give it a go, persuaded by their fans, the club and the media that they would be brilliant managers. Generally to be seen in tracksuits rather than a business suit.

  Kevin Keegan – popular, fragile, a great motivator and workaholic, he's still worshipped in Newcastle where his team so nearly won the Premiership. Now **retired from football**, he found that enthusiasm and hard work weren't enough for managerial success, especially when he was in charge of England. Best quote (and there are many to choose from): *'Chile have three options, they can either win or they can lose.'*

  Glenn Hoddle – never that popular (except maybe in Swindon and certain parts of London) and associated with some bizarre religious ideas, Hoddle is nonetheless recognised as a great team coach. After an up and down career in club management, he lost the England manager's job after saying: *'You and I have been physically given two hands and two legs and a half-decent brain. Some people have not been born like that for a reason. The karma is working from another lifetime.'* He's been wary of the media ever since. Blind MP David Blunkett said of the incident: *'If Glenn Hoddle is right then I must have been a failed football manager in a previous existence.'* Hoddle has recently denied saying these things, claiming lack of support from the senior people at the FA, who dropped him under pressure from the media.

- The **professorial** approach has been imported from Europe. These managers take a studious and intellectual view of the team, often standing back and allowing someone else to do the coaching for them. This managerial type is typified by these two managers...

    Sven Goran Eriksson – even though he looks like Mr Burns from *The Simpsons*, Eriksson has achieved remarkable success and that's just with the ladies. The glow that surrounded him when England beat Germany 5–1 has largely diminished (how's that for sports-journo-speak!?) and only a great World Cup will rescue his reputation. An expert in saying nothing but using a lot of words to say it.

    Arsene Wenger – Arsenal's studious French coach is famous not only for bringing Arsenal consistent success but also for his inability to see any incident where one of his players commits an offence. Must be lauded for his ability to get up the noses of the likes of Mourinho and Ferguson.

- The **old-school manager** is something of a rarity these days, mainly because so many mangers get sacked and it's a very stressful job, however here are two characters who sum up the way it should be done…

Graham Taylor – the 'failed' ex England manager has proved a great success at **club level**, sadly for him he's most famous for being cruelly portrayed as a turnip by *The Sun* newspaper and for the *Do I Not Like That* TV documentary.

Sir Bobby Robson – another ex England manager, with a hugely successful club career especially in Europe. Much loved, he has found a niche at the Republic of Ireland helping new manager, Steve Staunton. Best known for his memory lapses…When a news interviewer asked Newcastle's Shola Ameobi 'Do you have a nickname?' he replied, 'No, not really.' She went on to ask, 'So what does Bobby Robson call you?' 'Carl Cort,' came the reply.

Big Match Bingo – Manager's Speak

We were robbed	Boys done brilliant	Lessons learnt or learned	Take each game as it comes	Writing on the wall	Long way to go
Concentrate on the league/cup	Hairdryer	I didn't see the incident myself	Facing the inevitable	Caught a cold	A few more grey hairs
Consistency	Looking on helplessly	Hard graft	Good bunch of lads	Gamble	The boys got stuck in
Backing of the board	Grind out results	Positive thinking	When the right player comes along	All credit to…	No luck whatsoever
Honouring the contract	Stand up and be counted	Real character	Looking forward	The right balance	We just didn't want it enough

Just cross off six heard in any match commentary and shout 'Bingo!'

6

They Broke the Mould...
Brian Clough

'A genuine original.'

Pat Murphy, Brian Clough's biographer and friend

One of the Game's Great Characters

When it comes to originality and eccentricity one man stands out: Brian Clough. His comments about the game, chairmen, fellow managers and players stay with us like no other.

Something of a genius, Brian Clough was a highly successful player with Middlesbrough and Sunderland and he played for England twice, but had to cut his playing career short after a knee injury.

He first went into management at Hartlepool, becoming the youngest manager in the league; he had a couple of successful seasons there before moving to Derby County where he took them on to win the League Championship. Much to the fans' disgust, he was forced out of Derby where his style wasn't liked by the management, and after unsuccessful spells at Brighton and then Leeds (he was ousted by player power there) he ended up at Nottingham Forest. Under his leadership along with Peter Taylor Forest won promotion from the Second Division in 1977, and went on to win two European Cup titles, a League Championship and the League Cup on four occasions, although famously FA Cup success eluded him.

On the day of his last home game Forest were trying to avoid relegation – they lost the match, were relegated and he retired.

Despite the disappointment the Forest fans cheered him off. During the second half the away supporters started to chant his name, a moment that brought tears to his eyes and great credit to the travelling Sheffield United supporters.

Old Big 'Ead frightened the life out of the football establishment with his forthright views and eccentric management technique; he has left a legacy of entertaining quotes and observations. Here are some of the best...

On himself

- *'On occasions I have been big-headed. I think most people are when they get in the limelight. I call myself Big 'Ead just to remind myself not to be.'*

- *'I wouldn't say I was the best manager in the business. But I was in the top one.'*

- *'The River Trent is lovely, I know because I have walked on it for 18 years.'*

- *'I want no epitaphs of profound history and all that type of thing. I contributed. I would hope they would say that, and I would hope somebody liked me.'*

- *'Who thought Derby County could be turned into League champions; that any manager could bounce back from getting the bullet after 44 days with a great club and go on to prove himself among the best managers of all time; that what was*

THEY BROKE THE MOULD... BRIAN CLOUGH

done at Derby could be repeated at Forest; that after winning one European Cup, we could retain it; that a brash, self-opinionated young footballer, cut down by injury in his prime, would go on to achieve more impressive fame as a brash, highly successful manager?'

On fans

⚽ *'There are more hooligans in the House of Commons than at a football match.'*

On the England job

⚽ *'They thought I was going to change it lock, stock and barrel. They were shrewd because that's exactly what I would have done.'*

⚽ *'I might be an old codger now and slightly past my best as a gaffer, but the FA would know they're safe with me. At least I'd keep my trousers on.'*

On club chairmen

⚽ *'Football hooligans? Well, there are 92 club chairmen for a start.'*
⚽ *'If a chairman sacks the manager he initially appointed, he should go as well.'*

On Alex Ferguson

⚽ *'For all his horses, knighthoods and championships, he hasn't got two of what I've got. And I don't mean balls.'*

On players and their wives

⚽ *'That Seaman is a handsome young man but he spends too much time looking in his mirror rather than at the ball. You can't keep goal with hair like that.'*

⚽ *'Beckham? His wife can't sing and his barber can't cut hair.'*

⚽ *'Acne is a bigger problem than injuries.'* – On the young Forest team.

⚽ *'Players lose you games, not tactics. There's so much crap talked about tactics by people who barely know how to win at dominoes.'*

⚽ *'We talk about it for 20 minutes and then we decide I was right.'* – On dealing with a player who disagrees.

⚽ *'You got all those medals by cheating.'* – Endearing himself to the Leeds United players on his first day.

7

The Team, Teamwork and 'The Squad'

'We're taking 22 players to Italy, sorry, to Spain... where are we, Jim?'

Sir Bobby Robson on being asked whether Paul Gascoigne should have gone to the 1998 World Cup in France.

'Even when they had Moore, Hurst and Peters, West Ham's average finish was about 17th. It just shows how crap the other eight of us were.'

Harry Redknapp on his playing days.

It's a Team Sport…

We sometimes forget that football is a team sport and that most players and managers earn their keep without troubling the media too much. This team stuff comes with its own set of clichés and sayings that only come to the fore in football matches, so many of these can be applied equally to players as individuals, but we'll come onto that later in the book.

Here's a list of the best of them…

- **A job well done** – said when a team that is expected to win, wins by a close margin but without ever looking like they're in real trouble.

- **A lacklustre performance** – not poor, not great, but why use the word lacklustre? It only really applies when a team that is expected to play well doesn't. If it's really bad then commentators will say 'the wrong team turned up today' or 'the wrong team got off the coach.'

BIG MATCH BINGO

- **A professional performance** – probably the ultimate accolade to some managers and their teams as they win efficiently without incident and too much challenge, a **good work out for the team**.

- **A test of character** – any game that proves harder than expected or a tough game will be a test of character for the lads, usually associated with an English team going to somewhere like Istanbul. A test like this also **sorts out the men from the boys**.

- **Answering their critics** – applies to teams who have gone through a bad patch, usually when there's no real reason for it, having taken a lot of stick in the media. A good game enables them to **re-establish their credentials** and generally get back in everyone's good books.

- Any team involved in a **relegation battle** or **dog fight** will have to **dig deep** to show everyone **what they're made of** and **every match becomes a Cup Final**.

- **Aristocrats** – a team with pedigree with players that are technically excellent, they are great to watch and they probably hail from somewhere glamorous. It's applied to Spanish and Italian clubs, especially to the likes of Real Madrid.

- **Belied their lowly status** – said of a team that plays better than expected, usually against a bigger club in a cup game. In the tradition of most commentators and journalists it's said in that slightly patronising way they have when interviewing players from the **minnows**.

THE TEAM, TEAMWORK AND 'THE SQUAD'

- **Blend of youth and experience** – every successful team has that special blend of young players eager to make a name for themselves and **old stagers** who know the game and rely on experience to anticipate the opposition. Sometimes managers get away with having the balance in favour of older players, certainly Sam Allardyce and Harry Redknapp have successfully resurrected the careers of many an old has-been. With youth it's more difficult, but it can be done. As proven by Sir Alex Ferguson's Premiership-winning Manchester United team of the late Nineties, much to the chagrin of pundit Alan Hansen on *Match of the Day* who said of the team '*you can't win anything with kids*'.

- **Bragging rights** – one for derby games where there's nothing to win except the right to take the piss out of the losers and their fans.

- **Can they pick themselves off the floor?** – said after a particularly unjust incident or goal, if they do then it's all about their **character** and **temperament**. It will need **strong leadership**, **a plucky performance** and **a little luck to go their way**.

- **Claw their way back** – when a team is losing heavily or being dominated they occasionally **fight their way out of it**, or make a **remarkable comeback**, but mostly they seem to claw their way back. There are many examples of this but possibly the most memorable is Liverpool's amazing win over AC Milan at the European Championship Final in May 2005. Matches like this enable commentators to hit their cliché button and here are some examples from that match, from both online and on the radio…

At 3–0 down – *'If the Liverpool team was a dog, you'd shoot it at this stage.' 'Gerrard is useless and Kewell shouldn't have been allowed anywhere near a football pitch.'*

At half-time – *'Who are they trying to kid in England about the standard of football? Those Liverpool greats must be turning in their graves to see such a useless, lifeless performance. Sorry Bill, sorry Emlyn, sorry Tommy. Gerrard, you can't even think of walking in their shadows. Harry, go back to your Roos son, you are out of your class.'*

At 3–3 – *'Milan are gradually regaining composure after being rocked back on their heels by those three quick sucker-punches.'*

At the end of full time – *'Two halves, two totally different performances.'*

Liverpool win on penalties – *'Almost unbelievable.' 'History in the making.' 'Inspired by captain fantastic…'*

⚽ **Club versus country debate** – a familiar tale for great players from small countries who are under enormous pressure to stay at their clubs and not play for their country. Many feign injuries or just cave in under pressure from their club management who, after all, pay their wages. Premiership managers are fantastic whiners when it comes

THE TEAM, TEAMWORK AND 'THE SQUAD'

to this debate, especially over African players and the African Cup of Nations.

- **Collective unit** – rarely do managers praise one or two players after a match, it's always a **team effort**, and that success comes as a collective unit, not as a **bunch of individuals**.

- **Exhibition stuff** – when one team is so in control of a match and the level of skill they show is **out of the top drawer**. The danger is that this can lapse into showboating, which is always frowned upon as it shows disrespect apparently.

- **Final piece in the jigsaw** – usually applied to a player who has been brought in to perform a specific role within a team formation. The implication is that now, with him in place, the team will start winning... yeah right.

- **Fired up** – it's not good enough just to be motivated to do well, in football you must be fired up... or at the very least **up for it**. Woe betide any player who is perceived by the fans to be putting in less than 110 per cent (it's always 110 per cent, never 100 per cent). The manager will expect them to **get in there** and **show us what you're made of**.

- **Flying colours** – when any match is won and it's been a **tough game** then the team is said to have passed the test with **flying colours**. It's an old military term, a reference to coming off the battlefield with unit colours intact and flying, so quite apt sometimes.

- A contingent of foreign players in a team was once known as the **Foreign Legion**, but times have changed in the English game as evidenced by Real Madrid fielding more English players than Arsenal when they met earlier this year.

- **Heads went down** – this happens when it's obvious to the losing team that they have no way of winning, often being **totally outplayed** by the opposition. Of course, if they score then heads go up.

- **Hotbed** – any team that has lots of good players is a **hotbed** of talent, which is nice.

- **Kick start the season** – usually reserved for the autumn when a team has a bad start in the league, generally underperforms, then they suddenly have a win which **boosts confidence** and means a **march up the table**. This generally applies to Everton who seem to forget that they're actually a good side until they've played about ten games.

- **Lack of belief** – a common phrase from the losing manager, whose team either lack the confidence or mental strength to score a goal. The cumulative effect of several **poor results**.

- **Lacks a cutting edge** – a team without a decent strike force or the ability to create scoring opportunities for the strikers.

THE TEAM, TEAMWORK AND 'THE SQUAD'

- **Lads** – the collective name for the players is **the lads** as in 'there's a great set of lads in the dressing room', usually only said by English managers, not by the likes of Mourinho and Wenger. The 'lad' is usually said in a saddened tone and applies to a player who has usually tried something and failed e.g. 'all credit to the lad, but it just didn't work for him.'

- Any team that doesn't score regularly is described as **lacking quality in the final third** – that's final third of the football pitch not brain, although they are not mutually exclusive.

- **Line-up** – before a match the team is announced and this is where the team suddenly becomes the **line-up**. It may apply to the formation, whether it's a defensive or attacking line-up, and it's a pointer as to how they will play the game and how they will **set their stall out**.

- **Makeshift** – when **regular players** are missing, either through injury or suspension, the line-up is described as makeshift as it means that new players are drafted in from the reserves and some regulars have to **play out of position**, which is something their brains can't cope with easily. When the missing players return, it's always a **massive boost to the team**. Teams like Chelsea and Manchester United don't often field makeshift teams (unless it's on purpose, like for a Carling Cup match) as they have something most other teams don't have and that is **strength in depth**.

BIG MATCH BINGO

- **No more than they deserve** – said of a team who through endeavour and hard work finally get a goal, usually in the last quarter of the game.

- **On their day** – reserved for a team filled with great players or so it would seem **on paper** who, if things are going well for them – the weather is right, the pitch perfect and they're all in the right mood – **they begin to gel** and they are **well capable** of beating anyone.

- **Playing too narrow** – said of a team whose players seem incapable of getting out to the wings to make crosses. They often **over complicate things by playing through the middle**.

- **Route one merchants** – a team of rugged defenders, tall strikers and not much in the midfield, the ball is punted skywards towards the tallest striker who will **nod the ball down** for the striker's partner (usually diminutive and **nippy**) to score. Often associated with the **long ball** and **hit and hopers**, either way (to the annoyance of more sophisticated teams) it's very effective.

- **Strength in depth** – the province of the big Premiership clubs with their big squads and multi-talented players. Usually, during the match the commentator will point out the number of internationals sitting on the bench and say 'if only other clubs had that line-up to call on'.

- **Strong on paper** – is used to describe a team that looks

THE TEAM, TEAMWORK AND 'THE SQUAD'

good when you write the players' names down but who never seem to **live up to their billing**, at least not consistently.

- **Team goal** – a move that involves a number of players passing accurately culminating in a **well-worked** goal, no individual shines but it's the result of good teamwork and often a move **taken from the training ground**.

'I had 11 clubs – 12 if you count Stringfellows.'

Seventies icon and ladies' man Frank Worthington

Big Match Bingo – Team Stuff

Strength in depth	Route one	On their day	No more than they deserve	Massive boost to the team	Makeshift
Heads went down	Taken from the training ground	Kick start their season	Final piece in the jigsaw	Blend of youth and experience	Job well done
Totally outplayed	Fired up	Collective unit	Answer their critics	Aristocrats	When they begin to gel
Plucky	Good workout for the team	The lads	Professional	Lacklustre	Belie their lowly status
Well capable	Team effort	Lack of belief	Well worked	Bragging rights	Team goal

Just cross off six heard in any match commentary and shout 'Bingo!'

8

It's All About the Game...

'Football, it's a funny old game...'

Attributed to Jimmy Greaves and repeated by many others with the talent for stating the bleeding obvious.

'A game is not won until it is lost.'

David Pleat, now why isn't he managing a team these days?

Describing the Match

The job of the commentator is to describe to the viewers or listeners the game being played. This may sound obvious and easy, but for all of us who like to make out that their job is a lot more difficult than it really is, they have developed a language to **describe the action**.

Each game comes with its own set of problems and issues that need portraying as the match happens; here are the most over-used sayings and clichés…

- ☻ **A fair result in the end** – always said at the end of a match when everyone (with the possible exception of the managers, fans and players involved) agrees that the match result was a fair one considering the way the match was played. It's usually **a great advert for the game** as well.

- ☻ **Air of inevitability** – when a team is down on its luck and **results aren't going their way** games are played in an atmosphere where it seems inevitable that they are going to lose. Managers are sacked, players dropped and the local priest is called in to do an exorcism or something equally desperate.

☻ **At the death** is used to describe any incident that happens right at the end of a match; usually it's controversial which then makes it a **talking point** too.

☻ **Bore draw** is aptly used to describe any dull game that ends without a result. Maybe there should be a panel that adjudicates on the entertainment value of any game and deducts or adds points depending on how lively it is. In any boring match there comes a time when the commentator will ask the most talented player on the **park** to produce that **piece of magic** that will either **turn the game** or **break the deadlock**. If no one has scored then the commentator says that the game is **crying out for a goal** or mentions that the **game needs a goal**! In the unlikely event that the 0–0 is entertaining then the comment will be that it's **not your typical nil-nil**.

☻ Whenever a goal, shot or game is similar to one that went before the commentator will say that it was a **carbon copy of the last one**.

☻ Following an incident, a referee's crucial decision or a goal that is vital to the result, the commentator will say that it **changes the whole complexion of the game**.

☻ The term **clear water** comes up when a team goes ahead by two goals in a match, often there is then **daylight between**

IT'S ALL ABOUT THE GAME...

them, unless the other team **puts the cat among the pigeons** by **pulling one back**.

- **Consolation goals** are common when one team, in the process of thrashing another, lets in a goal as they relax, but funnily enough they are really no consolation to the team that scores it. Consolation goals can **take the gloss off** a win.

- **Encounter** is used when the commentator says game or match too often and feels like a change, having said that, it's never a ferocious game or ferocious match, it's always a **ferocious encounter**.

- **It's early days but…** is said when it appears that a match is going to turn out in a particular way. The Ronism here is **early doors** which is an old reference to pub opening times. It's allied to **there's a long way to go** which is usually said when a team scores early in a match, implying that there's plenty of time for the opposition to score. This then gives lie to the term **the first five minutes is crucial**.

- **Electric atmosphere** – part of the hype in any important match, a commentator must say that the atmosphere is electric even when it's not. If they can't get away with that they will mention how much noise the crowd makes, despite the low turnout. Matches played abroad, especially in countries like Turkey, are played in a **cauldron**.

- Commentators use **end-to-end stuff** to describe any game where the defence of both teams is rubbish and there's lots of attacking. Although **not one for the purist**, this type of match usually turns out to be a **good advert for the game** unless they are playing the **long ball game**, which is seen by commentators as effective but not quite in the spirit of the game (as it bypasses the best and most attractive players, those in midfield), unless it's genuinely exciting in which case they will say it's **pulsating**.

- **Epic** is used for the occasional **high quality encounter**, especially when the teams are from big clubs and the occasion demands it (e.g. at the World Cup). The lead must **change hands** a few times and the game must be **full of incident**.

- Any move where the passes come off as the players intend and everything goes to plan is called a **flowing move**, usually resulting in a **lovely goal**, which Stuart Hall would describe as **pure poetry**.

- **Game of two halves** – a classic football cliché, stemming from a match where one side dominates in one half while the opposition dominate in the second. A great example is Liverpool's Champions League win of 2005.

- **Game over** is said, usually by Andy Gray, as the goal is scored that **seals the fate** of the losing side.

- **Grind out, grind down the opposition** and **ground out a win** all imply that the game was won not by skill but by hard graft and tactics that **wore down the opposition** rather than dazzled them with skill. If the teams are evenly matched then it becomes a **hard fought battle** and if there's

IT'S ALL ABOUT THE GAME...

no winner then it's **honours even**. The players and managers usually say after the match **it wasn't pretty... but it's the result that matters**. Sod entertaining the paying fans then.

- Often the result of **one-way traffic**, the **icing on the cake** describes any goal that is taken with aplomb by a side already winning. The opposite of a consolation goal... rubbing it in, in other words. Any game that a side is dominating will invariably lead to the comment that it's **in the bag**.

- Any match where there are lots of bad tackles, **handbags** (minor scuffles), some fighting, or that involves Jens Lehmann is called an **ill-tempered affair**.

- **In the cauldron** is a term used to describe any hostile football environment, whether it's the stadium or the city where it's being held. Mainly used when any English club visits a Turkish one, then it's also often a **cauldron of hate**.

- Any goal scored late in a game that levels the match is a **last gasp equaliser**. Any goal scored very late in the game is scored **at the death**. In both cases they are scored with **virtually the last kick of the match**.

- Luck plays its part in most matches: teams will either (or not) get the **rub of the green** or the **run of the ball**. Whatever happens, most people involved in the game agree that **luck evens itself out through the course of a season**.

- Commentators and pundits, particularly Terry Butcher, love describing games in military terms. Favourites include battle, honour, up for the fight, out gunned, pulling the trigger, arsenal, all-out war, in the trenches, leading the line, leading the charge and walking wounded. Players that show great leadership or who are very committed will provoke the comment that the commentator would like them on 'our side' if there was a war.

- For commentators the **perfect time to score is a minute before half-time.**

- Good teams that get results by skill rather than brute force are often **entitled to an off day** when they **never got their passing game going** or **lacked belief.**

'That's going to happen a lot, teams will be at their most dangerous against us when we have the ball.'

Former Southampton manager Dave Jones

- Managers, especially international managers, always like to point out to interviewers that there are *no easy games these days.*

- Anything that is physical and unnecessarily punished by the referee usually results in the comment that they (or the authorities) have to understand that its **part and parcel of the game.**

IT'S ALL ABOUT THE GAME...

- ⚽ Cup competitions that are decided on penalties are generally disliked by commentators and ex player pundits. Described as a **penalty lottery**, it's often the most exciting part of the whole tournament.

- ⚽ All games are **influenced** by the **state of the pitch**. Commentators love banging on about the pitch, talking of conditions underfoot, how energy sapping it is and, if it's really bad, likening the pitch to a ploughed field which won't be **conducive to good football**. The pitch decides whether the game is played **on the deck** or **in the air** and it's usually responsible when a player misses badly. Then it **bobbles just before he hits it** and the player involved **looks at the ground accusingly**.

- ⚽ A team that scores more than their opposition **secures the win**. Commentators will add that they **secured the win courtesy of...** while any team that wins unjustly will be **flattered by the result**.

- ⚽ Commentators love bringing up past matches and games that have been a highlight before, so every time England play Germany there are **shades of '66**.

- ⚽ Whenever anyone wins anything it always **takes time to sink in**.

- ⚽ Whenever the crowd cheers in a big match the commentator says that the **crowd erupts**, which must be down to the electrifying atmosphere.

- The **form book goes out of the window** when a team that has been previously consistent suddenly loses to an **unlikely opponent**.
- Any team that is 2–0 down and scores is **thrown a lifeline** and that will make the last x number of minutes very interesting or bring the game to **an exciting climax**.

- Any game won by foul means or a penalty achieved by diving is described as a **travesty**, as is a poor refereeing decision that cruelly affects the result of the game.

- Any team that benefits from having an opposition player sent off never seems to make **full use of the extra man**.

- **Whoever scores first will win** is usually said when two opposing teams have particularly strong defences. Commentators have got wise to this as it usually signifies a dull game, meaning that the punters will start changing channels.

'I'm a firm believer that if the other side scores first you have to score twice to win.'

Howard Wilkinson, telling it like it is…

Big Match Bingo – It's a Funny Old Game…

There's a long way to go in this game	Early days or early doors	End-to-end stuff	Secures the win	Shades of…	On the deck
Lovely goal	Icing on the cake	Ill-tempered	Takes the gloss off	Battle	Long ball game
Electric atmosphere	Fair result in the end	Full of incident	Air of inevitability	Exciting climax	Bypass the midfield
Encounter	One-way traffic	Lacked belief	Unlikely opponent	Game needs a goal	Daylight between them
Grind out a win	At the death	State of the pitch	Break the deadlock	Form book	Talking point

Just cross off six heard in any match commentary and shout 'Bingo!'

9

Strachan

'There's nobody fitter at his age, except maybe Raquel Welch.'

Ron Atkinson

Gordon Strachan, the Bane of Stupid Interviewers

A hero on the terraces, the pitch and the internet, the Celtic manager deserves a mention for his abuse of the press – when it comes to dealing with stupid questions we have a champion.

- Gary Lineker: *So, Gordon, if you were English, what formation would you play?*
  Gordon Strachan: *If I was English I'd top myself!*

- Interviewer: *Welcome to Southampton Football Club. Do you think you are the right man to turn things around?*
  Strachan: *No. I was asked if I thought I was the right man for the job and I said, 'No, I think they should have got George Graham because I'm useless.'*

- Interviewer: *Is that your best start to a season?*
  Strachan: *Well, I've still got a job so it's far better than the Coventry one, that's for sure.*

- Interviewer: *Are you getting where you want to be with this team?*
  Strachan: *We're not doing bad. What do you expect us to be like? We were eighth in the league last year, in the Cup Final and we got into Europe. I don't know where you expect me to get to. Do you expect us to win the Champions League?*

BIG MATCH BINGO

- Interviewer: *Gordon, you must be delighted with that result?*
  Strachan: *You're spot on! You can read me like a book.*

- Interviewer: *This might sound like a daft question, but you'll be happy to get your first win under your belt, won't you?*
  Strachan: *You're right. It is a daft question. I'm not even going to bother answering that one. It is a daft question, you're spot on there.*

- Interviewer: *Bang, there goes your unbeaten run. Can you take it?*
  Strachan: *No, I'm just going to crumble like a wreck. I'll go home, become an alcoholic and maybe jump off a bridge. Umm, I think I can take it, yeah.*

- Interviewer: *There's no negative vibes or negative feelings here?*
  Strachan: *Apart from yourself we're all quite positive round here. I'm going to whack you over the head with a big stick, down negative man, down.*

- Interviewer: *Where will Marion Pahars fit into the team line-up?*
  Strachan: *Not telling you! It's a secret.*

- Interviewer: *You don't take losing lightly, do you, Gordon?*
  Strachan: *I don't take stupid comments lightly either.*

- Interviewer: *So, Gordon, in what areas do you think Middlesbrough were better than you today?*
  Strachan: *What areas? Mainly that big green one out there...*

⚽ Interviewer: *Gordon, can we have a quick word please?*
Strachan: *Velocity* [he then quickly walks off].

Quotes

⚽ *'I have discovered that when you go to Anfield or Old Trafford it pays not to wear a coloured shirt because everyone can see the stains as the pressure mounts. I always wear a white shirt so nobody sees you sweat.'*

⚽ *'Pahars has also caught every virus going except a computer virus and he is probably working on that even now.'*

⚽ On a comment that striker John Hartson is lazy… *'I did see a ginger, rotund guy out doing sprints in the car park this morning.'*

⚽ On old stagers Roy Keane and Neil Lennon for their performances during the 1–0 Old Firm win over Rangers: *'I thought Darby and Joan were excellent.'*

⚽ *'It's an incredible rise to stardom. At 17 you're more likely to get a call from Michael Jackson than Sven Goran Eriksson.'* On Wayne Rooney.

⚽ *'The world looks a totally different place after two wins. I can even enjoy watching* Blind Date *or laugh at* Noel's House Party.*'*

⚽ *'We even competed for the acne cream when we were younger. Obviously, I won that one.'* On playing with Alex McLeish.

⚽ *'I can see the loony hats being superimposed on me now but I still believe we can reverse it.'*

⚽ *'I've had better weeks. I tried to make it better by playing my dad at golf on Sunday. We played 13 holes and I got beat by a 60-year-old man with a bad limp. So hopefully bad things happen in threes and that will be the last of it.'*

⚽ *'If I was a centre-half and was having to put my head in and get cut, I would be saying to people out wide, "Don't allow these crosses or I'll come and knock your head off myself, you try being here for some of them".'*

Finally…

As an insight into what type of manager Strachan is, this is revealing…

> Strachan was on Sky on a Sunday morning. He saw John Terry's goal and said he was impressed that Terry goes up expecting to score. He contrasted this to Claus Lundekvam, the Saints' central defender who goes up for every dead ball and never ever looks remotely like scoring. He said if there was a dead body lying in the penalty area the ball would hit it on the head several times a season which, he commented, is more than Lundekvam can manage. He said referees should book Lundekvam for time wasting every time he goes up for a corner. When the co-commentator added that if Lundekvam was watching Strachan was only joking, Strachan assured him he was deadly serious.

10

Players

'I've told the players we need to win so that I can have the cash to buy some new ones.'

Chris Turner, Peterborough manager, motivating his squad.

'If my footballers were bricklayers the house they built would fall down.'

Alan Ball, World Cup winner and ex manager

The Lads

They are the lucky sods who get to play out the dreams of the supporters; they get handsomely rewarded (well some do); they are **high profile** celebrities and the commentators have got a whole host of sayings and clichés just for them.

- A good new player is always described as a **great acquisition** and a **wonderful addition** to the team; they may even **complete the jigsaw**, once they have **put pen to paper** and **pledged their future to the club** (at least until about 18 months before the contract is due for renewal anyway).

- The club badge is everything to some players and loyalty is seen as a precious commodity by the fans, it's rewarded with devotion, but woe betide any player who kisses the badge and feigns loyalty to the team, only to move on **when the opportunity arises**.

- Young players who come up through the club's youth team are a graduate of the **academy** or a result of forward thinking from the management. **Youngsters** are expected to be **learning all the time**, even if they do have an **old head on young shoulders**. It's OK for them to be **naive** but not **sloppy**.

- Once great and older players can still be **influential** and **instrumental** in the club's success, they may still have **that magic touch** occasionally and can be **on song** and **on their day** can still **set the game alight** (or **on fire** depending on the commentator) with **a collector's item**. Whatever happens **they aren't ready to hang up their boots** yet.

- Players who are particularly dynamic are praised for their **all-round contribution**, and set **very high standards** that **others can only follow**. A dynamic captain such as Bryan Robson in his prime is called **Captain Fantastic**; they are of course a **great ambassador for the game** and a **class act**.

- Those players at the **top of their profession** are the **finished article**, the **complete package** and **a joy to watch**. They are also possibly the **first name on the team sheet**. However skilful they may be it doesn't do to be **nonchalant** or disrespect the opposition by **showboating** – an **outrageous piece of skill** or **playing a blinder** is great but you can't be seen to be taking the piss. You can't be a **Champagne Charlie**.

- Sometimes though commentators and pundits (and us the fans) are just in awe of what really skilful players can do, it's probably summed up in Ray Clemence's comment about Gheorghe Hagi: *'Hagi could open a tin of beans with his left foot.'*

PLAYERS

- **Comfortable on the ball** is used by commentators when they are talking about big players, especially central defenders. It's always a surprise to them when anyone wearing a number five shirt is able to pass the ball accurately and not make a prat of themselves in the process.

- Commentators like to commend foreign players on their technical abilities (as though British players have none) and British players on their athleticism and passion (as though players from other countries are incapable of having those).

- **Quality** always tells or shines through in the end.

- Those players who have obvious skill are seen as **cultured** and if they favour particularly the left or right foot then the foot is cultured too, or **educated** if it's a midfield player, or **trusty** if they play anywhere else. Players who are equally adept with either foot have **two good feet**. They may be **equally at home** in any position but midfielders are often credited with **great vision** and the **ability to read the game**.

- The **consummate professional** is seen as a great accolade, particularly by the likes of Sky's Martin Tyler who often talks about **elite groups of players** who are **more than capable**. Some players are just **equipped to survive at this level** or become **journeymen** moving from club to club without being spectacularly successful; they are described as **honest** players who **ply their trade**.

- Big players are often said to have a **commanding presence**, especially central defenders and big centre forwards. Tall players are described as **leggy** and when they do something wrong to the fans they are become a **useless long streak of piss**. It's always thought that big men can't be skilful and commentators are always surprised when they **turn on a sixpence** to score. Whatever the occasion **they are always a handful** although there is often some confusion about the context in which this is meant, just look up Alex Ferguson's comments on Dion Dublin and you'll get the picture.

☻ Small or **diminutive** players are **busy**, if they show enough **commitment** to a commentator they can seem bigger than they really are.

☻ **Work rate, energy levels, industry** and a **good engine** are all admired qualities and it's always sad when a once speedy player (a **live wire**) loses that **yard of pace**, especially if they are not bright enough to make up for it with the ability to **anticipate the game** that **comes with experience**.

☻ Aggressive players are tolerated if they are not dirty with it, but it's often said that **off the pitch they are always a quiet lad**.

☻ **Complete turnip** is possibly associated with Graham Taylor when he was England manager, but it's become useful for those managers and pundits who want to describe a player's poor performance using 'acceptable' language. When players don't match up to their manager's expectations or they do something particularly stupid then they **did us no favours** is the term in vogue. Other terms you'll find are **they didn't perform** or **they went missing** or were **not**

PLAYERS

switched on, with the worst insult being **schoolboy error**.

- **He's like a fish out of water** usually signifies a drop down to the reserves.

- One of the worst crimes is for a player to be **anonymous** during a match, far better that they be described as **busy** even if they don't achieve anything much. Skilful players that just have an **off day** also have an **unusually quiet game** and managers **spare their blushes** by mentioning that the whole team is responsible.

*'I earn more than all you w******put together.'*
Attributed to Carlton Palmer, speaking to police after he was arrested during a night on the town.

- Players that show a never-say-die spirit are particularly loved by commentators, they look for the **unsung hero** and the **local lad** doing their bit for the cause. Showing bottle and being up for it are seen as ideal and particularly British qualities and highly competitive players who play with passion for the **whole 90 minutes** are praised to the hilt.

- It's traditional that when a player does something great he is modest about it and will always say that the lads gave him some stick about it. **Dressing room jokers** are also called **wind-up merchants**.

- At some stage in a match the manager will always want to

bring on his substitutes; commentators get very excited about this. If it's a **tactical switch** this provokes lots of debate about the options, a **like-for-like** change is a bit boring, but **bringing on fresh legs** is always entertaining as the new player may be **challenging for a spot in the team**, attempting to **make the shirt his own** and aiming to **cement his place**. The perennial substitute who has a habit of doing something special at the end of a match is called a **super sub**.

⚽ Hard men can be anyone, except possibly goalkeepers; they generally are **up for it** and **show a lot of bottle**. They don't go in for **heroics** but they are always **equal to the challenge** and eager to **renew their acquaintance** with their opposition.

Every position and playing area has developed its own set of terms and language and over the next few sections we'll explore the agony and the ecstasy of each…

'Ninety-five per cent of my language problems are the fault of that stupid little midget.'

           Gianfranco Zola on Dennis Wise's help with settling into the English game.

Big Match Bingo – the lads…

Super sub	Did us no favours	Energy levels	Finished article	Cement his place	Great ambassador for the game
Work rate	Went missing	Live wire	Outrageous piece of skill	Cultured	Complete package
Take no prisoners	Good engine	That extra yard of pace	Schoolboy error	Commanding presence	Renew their acquaintance
Heroics	Old head on young shoulders	Make the shirt his own	Educated	Class act	Unsung hero
Bottle	Solid in the air	Spare his blushes	Set the game alight	Real pro	Always a handful

Just cross off six heard in any match commentary and shout 'Bingo!'

11

Between the Sticks

'Football is a fertility festival, eleven sperm trying to get into the egg. I feel sorry for the goalkeeper.'

Bjork – singer and second most famous Icelander in the world of football.

Goalkeepers

Keepers are much maligned and generally abused; after all they are only really remembered for their mistakes (another cliché but it's a true one). They are always seen as slightly eccentric and a little unhinged and they like to project an image of uniqueness.

Eccentric goalkeepers abound, one of the most memorable being René Higuita, who not only sported the worst mullet/bobble perm ever seen on our shores, but performed the strange 'scorpion kick' save when he played for Columbia against England in 1996. As the ball came towards him he just jumped forward, arched his back and kicked the ball away with the soles of his feet. Surely it would have been easier to catch it, but then he is a goalkeeper.

Tragedy is never far away from the goalkeeper, just look at Werder Bremen goalkeeper Tim Wiese. After a brilliant display where everyone acknowledged he kept his team in the match, he dropped the ball (in a situation where he should have easily caught it) at the feet of an opposition player, who then scored. This was in the 88th minute of a European Championship match and had he not made the error his team would have been through to the last eight, possibly going on to meet the likes of Barcelona and creating riches for his club. Possibly the most expensive keeper error ever?

For those of us who are not Man U fans there was no better sight than seeing a completely pissed off Peter Schmeichel when they suffered a rare defeat. His face creased in disappointment, he appeared to take his frustrations out on his teammates by shouting at them very loudly, all this while his nose seemed to glow redder with every passing minute as the game ebbed away.

> *'Peter Schmeichel says that the present Man United team would beat the 1968 European Cup winners. He's got a point, because we're over 50 now.'*
>
> **Nobby Stiles**

It's traditional that in the very last minute of an important match the keeper acts as an outfield player and goes up to play his part in the last minute corner. On the final day of the 1998–99 season Carlisle United needed to win at home or lose their Football League status. With the score at 1–1 and well into injury time, Carlisle's on-loan goalkeeper Jimmy Glass ran the length of Brunton Park to score the winner from a corner with one second to spare. Carlisle was saved, but their owner still failed to give Glass a permanent contract.

So a good keeper can keep their team in the match (or better) while a poor one can lose it with one error – it's a vital position and probably one where the owners of the number one shirt don't get the credit they deserve. Yes, OK, I was a goalkeeper.

BETWEEN THE STICKS

> *'I was saying the other day how often the most vulnerable area for goalies is between their legs.'*
>
> **Andy Gray, Sky Sports**

Commentators have developed a set of phrases reserved just for the man **between the posts**. Here are a few choice examples you'll hear in virtually every match.

- Good goalkeepers have a **safe pair of hands**, they're **not afraid to catch the ball** and they are good at **cutting down the angles**.

- Goalies always like an **early touch** of the ball.

- Keepers like to **command their area**, dominating **the box** and coming **in early for crosses**, anticipating the play (**they have it covered**) before electing to **punch** or catch the ball.

- In any one-on-one situation they try to **make themselves big** and **cut down the angles**, or even **get their angles right** depending on the commentator.

- Acrobatic keepers are approved of, providing they don't show off and perform a dive **for the cameras**.

- Saves are **regulation** or **reaction** or **outstanding** depending on how close the striker is and how fast the ball is travelling in relation to the keeper's starting point. The best saves are always **world class**.

BIG MATCH BINGO

- **Goalmouth incidents** involve the goalkeeper and most of the defence; they are usually an **almighty scramble** resulting in a goal or a point when the keeper **clasps the ball to his chest**, usually **gratefully**.

- Shots that the keeper misses but then go on to hit either the post or the bar will bring the comment that the striker has been **denied by the woodwork** as though the goal is alive and capable of sentient thought, or able to physically move to save the shot.

- There comes a point in any one-sided game when the commentator will invariably mention that the losing side's keeper has been **the busier of the two keepers**.

- When a goal is scored (or **conceded**) the keeper usually makes **a despairing dive**, unless he gets lobbed, then he will either be in **no-man's land** or **way off his line**.

- When a keeper **comes for the ball** he doesn't just catch it, he **smothers the ball**.

- **Straight down his throat** is used to describe shots directly at the keeper, said as though it's a complete mystery as to why the striker did that.

- Obviously the goalie's job is to keep a **clean sheet** and when this happens over a long period the commentary team will start counting up the minutes since the last goal was conceded. The record as we go to print is by Abel Resino of

Atlético Madrid, with 1275 minutes in 1991, so roughly 16 minutes into his 15th match.

'Somewhere in there the grace of a ballet dancer joins with the strength of an SAS squaddie, the dignity of an ancient kind, the nerve of a bomb disposal officer.'

Some pretentious bollocks about being a goalkeeper from author and ex player Eamonn Dunphy.

12

At the Back

'The only people I can exonerate are the six [players] I left on the bus – they wouldn't want to be anywhere near anything like that – and the two boys up front. Maybe I should have played them at the back.'

Alan Curbishley, after a 4–1 loss

Defence

When it comes to the Premiership Sunderland have the worst defensive record, with the class of 2002/3 being the worst of all, despite their latest debacle. It seems that some managers think that buying attackers is the best policy, ignoring the fact that you have to stop the other team scoring as well; some even make a tradition out of it, just think Newcastle Utd or even Real Madrid.

Commentators generally admire plucky defenders who show lots of spirit and a never-say-die attitude, for example Bobby Moore and Terry Butcher. They love to hate cynical defenders, especially so if they are Italian – the most disliked was probably Franco Baresi, but special bile is reserved for any Argentinean defender.

> *'The good news for Nigeria is that they're two-nil down very early in the game.'*
>
> **Kevin Keegan, summarising brilliantly at the last World Cup.**

Defenders make the dourest TV pundits with Alan Hansen being the best known and possibly the most direct, as when he described Denmark's 4–1 thrashing of England as: *'an absolute shambles. Communication, organisation and man-marking was nil'*.

BIG MATCH BINGO

His favourite words and phrases such as **shocking**, **shambles** and **naive defending** (allied to his Scottish accent) are classics, and no book such as this would be complete without them.

However, there's much more to defending than Hansen and here are the commentator's classics when describing the work of the men at the back...

- Naivety can possibly be forgiven but when it comes to lousy defending it's about **compounding the agony** or **misery**. Mix-ups in **the box** or **crowded area** are either a **catalogue of errors** or **comedy of errors** depending on the situation.

- It's boring but generally the teams with the best defenders are the most successful.

- Own goals (usually called a **sickener**) are always a highlight for any neutral and benefiting team, especially the bit when the camera focuses on the unfortunate who has just scored. Sometimes you just have to laugh, whichever side you're rooting for.

- Another commentary favourite is **you can drive a coach and horses through that defence**, which is great, but whatever the situation you can guarantee that the defenders will have **lost their men** and be guilty of **ball watching**.

AT THE BACK

'It was like they parked the team bus in front of the goal!'

Jose Mourinho, after a 0–0 draw with Tottenham.

- ⚽ The under-hit back pass is a chance for both comedy and tragedy to shine either way; it's a chance for commentators to ask **what's he doing?** Or observe that the culprit is **far too casual** or point out a **lack of communication** between defender and keeper. **He should have given him a shout.**

- ⚽ Under-hit balls are generally known as **hospital passes** as the defender and attacker have no choice but to go for the ball, usually leaving one of them injured or at least feigning injury (by rolling around theatrically).

- ⚽ Tackles can be, at the most extreme, **career ending**, with the **two-footed challenge** being the worst. Hard defenders **leave their calling cards** without injury, just letting the opposition know they are in a tough game. The worst crime is for a defender to **pull out of a challenge** and **bottle it**.

'Had we had another injury to one of our central defenders, I would have had to put a fullback in there — and neither of them can head the ball!'

Harry Redknapp on a shortage of fit players.

- **Ugly challenges** where one player **clatters into** another do little harm but look bad, much better to get a **timely intervention** with **an outstretched leg**.

- At some point in a match someone will **fall awkwardly** or there will be a **clash of heads**.

- **Cynical fouls** are less common now, although the **cynical block** is still **part and parcel of the game**.

- Players who defend well are always **immense** or a **colossus**, they **lead by example** and there's always a point in the game when the commentator will say that **they are everywhere** or that **the ball follows them**.

- Hansen likes **no-nonsense defending** even if sometimes it's a bit **agricultural** and the ball **ends up in row Z** – it's about getting the ball away from the goal, it doesn't matter how you do it. The opposition must be **dealt with, closed down, not given time and space**, with all the team doing their bit.

'Poland nil, England nil, though England are now looking the better value for their nil.'

Commentator Barry Davies

- These days all players are expected to play their part in defending and the defensive midfield player has emerged as a key part of any successful team. Their job is to **sit in**

AT THE BACK

front of the back four or **snuff out attacks before they happen.**

- Every defender has to guard against diving; some forwards are so skilled at it that it really seems that they have been fouled, others have the acting ability of a peanut and roll around the floor like they've been **pole-axed**. The mystery of it is that referees still fall for it.

- Woe betide any midfield player who doesn't **track back**, especially if the man he is supposed to be marking **goes on to score**.

'I was at a social function with him the other week, and it's the first time I've got within ten yards of him and he hasn't kicked me. Even then I kept looking over my shoulder...'

Kevin Keegan on defender Romeo Benetti.

Big Match Bingo – Keeping the Sheet Clean

Clean sheet	Hard man	Immense	Safe pair of hands	Timely intervention	Calling card
Lack of communication	Ball watching	Shambles	Naive defending	Crowded area	Closing down
Command the area	Almighty scramble	Saved his blushes	Goalmouth incident	Not given time on the ball	Sickener
Comedy of errors	Compounding the agony/misery	Bottle	Despairing dive	Denied by the woodwork	Catalogue of errors
One for the cameras	Elect to punch/catch	Hospital pass	Far too casual	Time and space	No-man's land

Just cross off six heard in any match commentary and shout 'Bingo!'

13

On the Charge

'One day, someone will end a football game scoring more than Brazil. This might be the time that they lose!'

Sir Bobby Robson

> *'What makes this game so delightful is that when both teams get the ball they are attacking their opponent's goal.'*
>
> **Jimmy Hill, showing a level of insight so commonly seen among pundits.**

On the Attack

In most attacks built-in defence comes from talented midfield players whose job it is to set the ball up for the forwards to score the goals. It used to be that simple, but now midfield players are classed by commentators as either defensive or attacking, but thank God for good old fashioned wingers and Andy Gray, who uttered the immortal line: *'For my money, Duff, servicing people from the left with his balls in there is the best option.'*

Like all areas of the game the midfield comes in for its own selection of commentary clichés…

- ☻ Some midfielders have the job of trying to win the ball before it gets to the defenders; it's important that they have great stamina, or a **good engine**. Players like Roy Keane and Bryan Robson get labelled **all action** and are praised for their ability to **get up and down the park**, covering **every blade of grass**.

'We reckon Carlton covers every blade of grass, but then you have to if your first touch is always that crap.'

Former Southampton manager Dave Jones on Carlton Palmer after a heavy defeat.

- It's crucial that the midfielder is a **ballplayer** with **good vision**, as the team relies upon their ability to **distribute the ball**, usually **down the channels** or **into the path** of the attacker for him to **latch onto**. Sometimes it's a **cunning ball** which **cuts out the last defender**.

- Creative midfielders have to be adaptable and have **two good feet**.

- The **midfield general** controls the game, his weapons being the **killer ball** and the **slide rule pass**; whatever he does it has to be **quality**.

Strikers come in all shapes and sizes with Paul Dickov at one extreme and Peter Crouch at the other, and providing they keep scoring it's a good life. They must have **composure in front of goal**, a **poacher's instinct**, the ability **to lose their man** and be able to **hit the target**.

Commentators hanker after a good old fashioned centre forward, usually in the mould of gap-toothed Joe Jordan, a proper **target man**. Someone who can bring the ball down and keep it while the rest of the team catch up is **willing** and will **work his socks off** for the team.

Foreign forwards, with the exception of Thierry Henry (who is near sainthood in the eyes of most commentators), are typically seen as a little weak, technically brilliant but with the tendency to **go down too easily**. Diving is generally frowned upon, except when an England international goes down in the box, then it's **part and parcel** of the game.

> ***'Tell the Kraut to get his ass up front. We don't pay a million for a guy to hang around in defence.'***
>
> **Allegedly uttered by a New York Cosmos executive, on Franz Beckenbauer's positioning.**

Here then are the commentator's favourites when it comes to the art of goal scoring, or at least attempting to score…

- ⚽ The easiest of attempts is a **tap-in**, which usually occurs after a flowing move or a goalmouth scramble. Some players have been known to miss from a few feet away, usually with an open goal in front of them — there are many examples: Ryan Giggs missing **a sitter** in a crucial game against Arsenal a couple of years ago, and Ronnie Rosenthal's spectacular shot from a few yards away which bounced off the crossbar are just two that come to mind. As the commentator often says — **it would have been easier to score.**

- ⚽ When a usually efficient and proficient striker scores the commentator will invariably remark that **he doesn't miss**

BIG MATCH BINGO

from there, the player in question then invariably does just that ten minutes later.

- **Creating chances** is what it's all about but you have to **convert** them too. Chances can be **gilt-edged, gift-wrapped** or **glorious**.

- Pace is the one thing that **really frightens defenders** and that's OK as long as the pacey player isn't too **one dimensional**.

- If a player somehow **contrives to miss** the goal as though some mysterious force is involved other than himself, he'll look at the ground or his teammates for consolation; meanwhile sympathetic commentators will say that the **ball bobbled up as he hit it** or that it was a **difficult chance** that **could have gone anywhere**. Those not so charitable will observe that he **couldn't hit a cow's arse with a banjo**... Virtually all missed chances end with the comment... **he should have scored**.

- Hitting the woodwork is deemed unlucky, a good try, but ballooning the ball over into row Z usually results in at least a few jeers, more if it's a top player.

- The **long-range effort** usually results in the ball being lodged somewhere by the corner flag, but if the striker makes **good contact** with the ball and really **lets fly** then the **goalkeeper will be tested**. It's always good to do this **early on** but shooting **straight down the goalie's throat** isn't advisable – both from the footballing and medical points of view.

ON THE CHARGE

- Shots come in all shapes and sizes, but once the striker **pulls the trigger** it can be **unerring** or **rasping**, **net-busting** or like a **thunderbolt**. Sometimes they are **a pearler** or a **sizzler**, but if on target they will all be judged as **no mean effort**. Attempting to lob the goalie is always described as an **audacious** or an **ambitious chip**.

'If you're in the penalty area and don't know what to do with the ball, put it in the net and we'll discuss the options later.'

Liverpool managerial genius Bob Paisley

- If a free kick is given just outside the box, the commentator in an England match, for example, will mention that it's **within Beckham territory**. If Beckham misses with his first couple of attempts, then on the third one the commentator will say that he's had a couple of **sighters** to get his range. Elaborate free kicks always elicit the comment that it was **straight off the training ground**.

- Some players, such as Roberto Carlos, have the reputation for having a hard shot; **a good shot on him** or a **thunderous left foot** are two comments specially trotted out when one of these guys lines up a free kick. He'll **pack a hell of a punch** too.

- It doesn't do to be too ambitious in front of goal, there's nothing more embarrassing than a failed overhead kick or an **air shot**. Being **caught in two minds** results in a **cross-shot** or a **cross-cum-shot**.

- Being **caught on the break** is a **nightmare** for most teams, especially those that have **committed men up front**.

- Headers are usually **strong, cushioned** or a **bullet**. A **free header** happens when a player gets to head the ball while being unmarked – why you don't get a free shot is a mystery.

- To a striker making the **net bulge** provides his **bread and butter**, he must **make no mistake** and finish with aplomb for the fans, **wheeling away** in celebration.

- A great goal is something to be celebrated, a real **collector's item** which, when it happens on Sky, will ensure that Andy Gray says 'take a bow, son' or 'pick that one out'.

- Sky, and Andy Gray in particular, have an obsession with pace, 'it's the one thing defenders are frightened of'. Attacking players who are fast but not exceptionally so, are described as having **a bit of pace**, those slightly faster are called **pacy**, while those who are fastest can **skin** the opposition with pace or can be **electrifying, genuine, remarkable, frightening, lightning** or even **unbelievable**. Sometimes though they just have **pace to burn**.

- Athletic defenders are always praised by commentators for their ability to keep up with a fast-paced **front man**, as though it's a just a coincidence that they happen to be able to run fast as well.

- Teams and players on form will be **scoring for fun** with players **queuing up** to score, ready to **open their account** and to score a **hatful of goals**, with their opposition having **no answer** for them.

- If there are plenty of attacks, lots of shots and yet no one can **squeeze a goal**, then the goal will be **leading a charmed life**.

- Those in the middle of a **goal drought** will be **asking themselves where the next goal is coming from** and generally **looking to the heavens**, hoping their luck will change.

Big Match Bingo – On the Attack!

Open goal	Goal drought	Caught on the break	Finish with aplomb	Ball bobbled up	Straight off the training ground
Cross-cum-shot	Rasping	Sitter	Free header	Down the channels	Sighter
Long-range effort	Hatful of goals	Scoring for fun	Tap in	Composure in front of goal	Pacey
Woodwork	Gilt-edged	Gift-wrapped	Glorious chance	Latch onto	Goes down too easily
Committed too many men up front	One-on-one	Make no mistake	Wheeling away	Caught in two minds	Air shot

Just cross off six heard in any match commentary and shout 'Bingo!'

14

The Wit and Wisdom of the England Manager

'Being an ex England manager, one that failed to qualify for the World Cup, is like being a dead politician.'

Graham Taylor

The Top Job

The England manager's position is seen as one of the top jobs in the game with, in theory at least, the best managers getting the job. They used to be sensible, hard-working men like Alf Ramsey or Ron Greenwood, but ever since Don Revie we seem to have picked a bunch of eccentrics, so here are some examples of the wit and wisdom of previous incumbents...

On the job

- *'For some it's the ultimate job, for the others it's the last job.'* Kevin Keegan with excellent powers of observation.

- *'I don't travel around the world with a school class; I'm not a school-teacher or the father of a Sunday School.'* – Sven Goran Eriksson

- *'The only way I will leave this job will be because of results. I'm too stubborn to quit because of criticism – too stubborn.'* – Sven Goran Eriksson

- *'Even now a team of linguists is at work translating Don Revie's writings on the game [of football] from the original gibberish into Arabic.'* – Michael Parkinson on the England manager's decision to take a job in the Middle East.

On luck

- *'Napoleon wanted his generals to be lucky. I don't think he would have worked with me.'* – Graham Taylor

On the fans

- *'England have the best fans in the world and Scotland's fans are second-to-none'* – Kevin Keegan

On options

- *'I have a number of alternatives, and each one gives me something different.'* – Glenn Hoddle

- *'There are two schools of thought on the way the rest of this half is going to develop; everybody's got their own opinion...'* – Kevin Keegan

Getting obscure

- *'At this moment in time I did not say them things.'* – Glenn Hoddle

- *'I never heard a minute's silence like that.'* – Glenn Hoddle

- *'The greatest barrier to success is the fear of failure.'* – Sven Goran Eriksson getting deep.

WIT AND WISDOM OF THE ENGLAND MANAGER

- *'I would have given my right arm to be a pianist.'* – Sir Bobby Robson

- *'I'll never play at Wembley again, unless I play at Wembley again.'* – Kevin Keegan

- *'I had mixed feelings – like watching your mother-in-law drive over a cliff in your car.'* – Terry Venables

- *'If history repeats itself, I should think we can expect the same thing again.'* – Terry Venables

On the opposition

- *'We didn't underestimate them. They were a lot better than we thought.'* – Sir Bobby Robson on playing Cameroon.

- *'England can end the millennium as it started – as the greatest football nation in the world.'* – Kevin Keegan

- *'Argentina won't be at Euro 2000 because they're from South America'* – Kevin Keegan showing his knowledge of geography.

- *'They're the second best team in the world, and there's no higher praise than that.'* – Kevin Keegan

On players

- *'Titus looks like Tyson when he strips off in the dressing room, except he doesn't bite. And he has a great tackle.'* – Sir Bobby Robson on his player's attributes.

⚽ *'I don't think there's anyone bigger or smaller than Maradona.'* – Kevin Keegan

⚽ *'What can I say about Peter Shilton? Peter Shilton is Peter Shilton, and he has been Peter Shilton since the year dot.'* – Sir Bobby Robson on the longevity of the England goalkeeper.

⚽ *'They compare Steve McManaman to Steve Heighway and he's nothing like him, but I can see why – it's because he's a bit different.'* – Kevin Keegan

⚽ *'When he plays on snow, he doesn't leave any footprints.'* – Don Revie on Leeds and Scotland midfielder Eddie Gray.

⚽ *'Just because I play for England, he thinks I understand peripheral vision and positive running.'* – Jimmy Greaves on England manager Walter Winterbottom.

The 'you know', 'to be fair' and 'obviously' records...

⚽ *'You know…'* – Wayne Rooney – 15 times in one interview, March 2006.
⚽ *'To be fair…'* – Peter Beardsley – 28 times in one commentary, October 2002.
⚽ *'Obviously…'* – Bryan Robson – ten times in one interview, December 2001.

15

The Romance of the Cup

'And I honestly believe that we can go all the way to Wembley... unless somebody knocks us out.'

Dave Bassett

The Cup Runs

The media love cup competitions, they like to bring out the history of the tournament and remind us of past glories, the romance and the tragedies. To do this they have created a whole new set of phrases and clichés just for the occasion.

- ☻ The FA Cup is always romantic and commentators go all misty-eyed as they play reruns of **giant killing exploits**, such as when Ronnie Radford scored from over 30 yards for Hereford United to knock out **the mighty** Newcastle. **It brings a lump to the throat, Brian.**

- ☻ **Concentrate on the league** – a classic, to be said after being knocked out of an important cup competition. The league position is always given more importance than winning a cup by the media and management, but the fans know that for most clubs, league position rarely changes that much and a cup is what they really want.

- ☻ As usual **the minnows** have the chance to play **the big boys** (with their **big guns**) and the opportunity to **cause an upset**, and whatever the result it becomes a **big pay day** that **guarantees the small club's future**.

BIG MATCH BINGO

- Big clubs drawn against **tricky opponents** from the lower divisions face being **dumped from the competition** after slipping on **a potential banana skin**.

- With the exception of Chelsea (whose pitch is the football equivalent of a ploughed field) the generally poorer pitches at smaller clubs are seen as a **great leveller** when it comes to them coping with the talents of the big clubs.

- It's all in the **luck of the draw** and a draw is what commentators like to avoid as it means the **lottery of penalties**, which they always say 'none of us want to see'. What they fail to appreciate is that for most fans (**the neutrals**) it's the most exciting bit.

- In tournaments like the Champions League much is made of the exoticism of the clubs we play from other countries and they come with their own sets of clichés...

  - *Real Madrid* – awesome talent; not won anything for ages; surprising how good Beckham actually is; guessing who the next manager is likely to be.
  - *Milan* (both clubs) – usually attempt to pronounce it Meelan and then revert back to the usual pronunciation after a few minutes. Reruns of past glories and close-ups of fans that have eaten too much pasta.
  - *Barcelona* – more awesome talent; worship at the feet of Ronaldinho and suggest that the goal he scored against England at the World Cup was a fluke.
  - *Galatasaray* – violent fans; cauldron of hate etc. etc.

ROMANCE OF THE CUP

- ⊗ *Bayern Munich* – (or any German club for that matter) shades of '66; 5–1; boring and efficient.
- ⊗ *Any other European club* – they are just not worthy so will be patronised.

- ⊛ European competitions mean that there will always be mention of **the priceless away goal** and how important defending is in Europe.

- ⊛ In competitions with a league system there's always a group which is more competitive that the others and this is always referred to as the **group of death**.

Big Match Bingo – Full Time

Unexpected result	Can you pick yourself up from this?	They didn't deserve it	I didn't see the incident myself	No way it was a penalty	Lacklustre performance
The ref had a poor game	The lads have got to take a long, hard look at themselves	It wasn't pretty… it's the result that matters	Virtually the last kick of the match	A bad day at the office	A few more grey hairs
Heads went down	Plucky performance	Remarkable comeback	Team effort	Bore draw	Fair result in the end
At the death	Talking points	A good advert for the game	Icing on the cake	As predicted	Full of incident
Ill-tempered	Lacked belief	Never got their game going	Lessons learned	Players went missing	Players have to hold their hands up
Takes time to sink in	A job well done	Answered their critics	Just reward	All credit to…	Outstanding

Just cross off six heard in any match commentary and shout 'Bingo!'

16

National Pride

'You've beaten them once. Now go out and bloody beat them again.'

Part of Alf Ramsey's pep talk to England before the 1966 final.

'John Harkes going to Sheffield, Wednesday'

Headline in the New York Post in 1993.

Internationals, Foreign Players and National Teams...

It's probably true to say that other than a few people at FA and SFA headquarters most people think 'friendlies' are a waste of time, though occasionally they do **throw up a good** match, such as when England played Argentina recently.

You can rely on our commentators to come up with a bagful of clichés and the usual borderline-xenophobic received wisdom about foreign players and national teams. Here, by country, is what they normally come out with...

The Spanish

- Highly talented but don't convert that talent into results.
- Tournament failures – perennial quarter finalists (a bit like England then).
- Passionate fans, overtones of racism.
- Divers, great at playacting.
- Latin temperaments.

The Italians (the Azzuri)

- Efficient but brittle.
- Technically excellent.
- Lost the plot in recent years.
- Passionate fans, overtones of Nazism.
- Have a game plan based on tight defence and well-placed fouls. Known in Italy as the *Catenaccio* meaning door bolt.
- Latin temperaments, front players usually too good-looking by half, defenders all ugly.
- Always someone's dark horse for the tournament.

The Germans

- Always **rise to the occasion**.
- Dodgy haircuts. (A mullet haircut is called a *bundesliga* in the Czech Republic.)
- Athletic, hard to beat and ruthless.
- Get lots of penalties.
- Commentator will always mention '66 and 5–1.

The French

- Gallic pride.
- Their cooking.
- Sublime skill, ageing team.
- Past glories.
- They all play in the Premier League.
- How good-looking they are.

NATIONAL PRIDE

The Argentineans

⚽ Generally hated, grudgingly admired, commentators can barely contain themselves.

The Brazilians

⚽ Can do nothing wrong.
⚽ Every neutral's favourite
⚽ Play with such freedom.
⚽ Love their football.
⚽ Past glories.

Everyone else

⚽ Australia, Poland, Norway and Sweden – England's **bogey teams.**
⚽ Commentators quite like the Irish, Dutch and the Portuguese because they generally over-perform or play attractive football while losing gloriously.
⚽ Central and South American (other than Argentina and Brazil) – generally seen as vaguely interesting with some coverage given if there are Premiership players involved.
⚽ African sides – as for South American but they have slightly more prominence as many of the players speak English and play in the Premier League.
⚽ Asian teams – generally patronised, except South Korea and Japan.

- Middle Eastern teams – rarely get a mention, no credibility at all.
- North American and West Indian teams – begrudging respect for the USA but patronising elsewhere (**good to see them involved**, comments about their lack of funds etc.).

General 'Comments' Associated with Internationals

- There are **no easy games anymore**.
- Teams **come here to defend**.
- Are friendlies worth the effort?
- Friendlies – tedious, **humdrum affairs**.
- Managers whinge about losing players on **international duty**.
- Everyone griping about the number of substitutions.
- We all wonder how Sven or Walter can learn much from friendly internationals.
- **Lesser nations** – teams from small countries or ones where football isn't the national sport (try asking who David Beckham is in India); this term is usually partnered with 'there are no more easy games in football' or 'even the smallest nation can get nine men behind the ball'.

Paul Gascoigne, on being asked on live television if he had a message for the people of Norway... 'Yes, f**k off...'

NATIONAL PRIDE

Clichés and Quotes from Overseas…

Below is a selection of foreign football clichés and names for moves, tricks and stuff that is just peculiar to that country.

The **nutmeg** is admired everywhere and each country seems to have its own idiosyncratic term…

- *Tunneln* – Germany.
- *Gurkerl* – meaning gherkin in Austria.
- *Le petit pont* – French, means little bridge which sort of makes sense, *le grand pont* is the trick of knocking the ball to one side of an opponent and then nipping around the other side to collect it.
- *Kötény* – Hungarian for apron?!
- *Cañas* – meaning 'drinking straw' in Brazil.
- *Panna* – meaning door or gate in Holland.

Other tricks and methods for getting the ball around the opponent seem to bring out a rash of sayings mainly to do with scarves, sombreros and hats!

Goooooooaaaaaaaallllllll!! Is the usual reaction to a goal by Latin American commentators who will usually string the word out as long as there is breath in their lungs to do so. More recently this has been replaced by the more entertaining '*Gol, Gol, Gol…*' – repeated over and over it can last much longer than just extending the word.

Overseas fans, players, managers and commentators are not above the odd weird comment or moments of bitchiness…

- The Portuguese obviously have hang-ups about skilful players whose **end product** comes to nothing: they are said to 'play in the sand' *(brinca-na-areia)* or get known as 'a triathlon player' *(jogador triatlo)*.

- The Spanish, meanwhile, get obsessed about the dark side, a poor game is 'boring to the death' *(aburren a los muertos)* or 'on the brink of ruin' *(al borde del abismo)*.

  Other Spanish commentary classics are:

    - *Eso es futbol arte y alegria...* it is football, art and happiness.
    - *Fenomeno...* genius.
    - *Enorme...* great.
    - *Son un lujo...* they are a luxury.
    - *Perdona y regala...* forgive and give free.

- In answer to the question what did he, as a Roman, think of the slogan 'carpe diem' (seize the day), Italian star Francesco Totti is said to have replied: *'What's that shit, I don't speak English.'*

- Of course some players can be stereotypical in their actions – take French star Nicolas Anelka who, in an obvious case of ego triumphing over talent, said to his national coach Jacques Santini: *'You'll have to get on your knees and beg before I play for you again.'*

- Just to prove that it's not just European football that's full of clichés and poor grammar, here's a match description

NATIONAL PRIDE

from an Egyptian soccer site: *'Al Ahly won crumbled and title holders Zamalek in less than ten minutes with three goals to nul in the main match of the Egyptian league's 20th week, which was mostly a dull match, goals were from Emad Motaab and Abo Trika who scored two goals. Ahly now is officially the new title holders of the Egyptian League champions after a drought that lasted 4 years.'*

- *'Love is good for footballers, as long as it is not at half-time.'* – Richard Moller Nielsen, Denmark coach.

- *'I should have been born English. When I hear "God Save the Queen" it can make me cry. Much more than I cry when I hear "La Marseillaise". I think Thierry Henry is a bit like me – he understands the English mentality. He gets it.'* – Eric Cantona endearing himself to his countrymen.

- *'We can't behave like crocodiles and cry over spilled milk and broken eggs.'* – nonsense from Italian coach Giovanni Trappatoni.

- Showing a talent for the bleedin' obvious...

    - *'If you want to score a goal, you have to hit the target.'* – Fabio Capello
    - *'Sometimes in football you have to score goals.'* – Thierry Henry
    - *'We lost because we didn't win.'* – Ronaldo

- *'My granddad wants his bicycle back!'* A chant sung by Dutch fans to the Germans, whose troops confiscated Dutch bicycles during WW2.

⚽ Some modest classics from the master of Dutch football, Johan Cruyff...

- ⚽ *'What is speed? The sport press often takes speed for insight. Look, if I start to run earlier than somebody else, I look faster.'*
- ⚽ *'Lots of people see that during a match something goes wrong and only very few see what you can do about it. Yes, I see that immediately.'*
- ⚽ *'I was always a professional, I have always been thwarted. I was constantly surrounded by amateurs, who frustrated me in my idealism.'*
- ⚽ *'Yes I am indeed someone who doesn't want to fiddle. I set my own laws and they don't get altered very quickly. I can be tough in that.'*
- ⚽ *'To start with there is only one ball and that is the one to have, but what you do with that ball? That is what matters.'* (No wonder he was hailed as a genius.)
- ⚽ *'Bad luck is the result of a negative attitude, good luck of a positive attitude.'*
- ⚽ *'Italians cannot win from you, but you can lose from them.'*
- ⚽ *'If you become champion with ten points difference, you can't take them with you to the next season.'*

The Germans

As the World Cup is played in Germany this year we thought we'd do a special section just on their best clichés, quotes and general dumbness...

NATIONAL PRIDE

- In France and Germany the team at the bottom of the league carry the red lantern (which appeared on the back of the last carriage of a train) – *la lanterne rouge* and *rote laterne*.

- In Germany negative play is called *anti-fußball*, a term which would describe some UK-based clubs well. While an 'English week' (*Englische woche*) describes a week in which a team plays both at the weekend and midweek.

- The Germans have other great descriptive terms, with my favourites being *rowdyhaft*, an excellent term for behaving like a hooligan, and *stink finger*, which is the middle-fingered salute popular in the US.

- Just to show that there's no hard feelings and that 'shades of '66' happen in German too a 'Wembley goal'(*Wembleytor*) is one that is awarded even though the ball didn't cross the line.

- For bitterness the prize has to go to Berti Vogts who said when managing Scotland: *'If I walked on water, my accusers would say it is because I can't swim.'* He also said: *'I believe that the team at the top of the table can beat the front runner any time.'* While the Germans' most successful domestic coach, Udo Lattek, had this excuse lined up – *'The defence is afraid of their weak keeper, that's why they play so well.'*

- A rare German joke – Definition of a man: A human being who will purchase soccer tickets three months in advance, but waits until Christmas Eve to buy Christmas presents.

- The Germans' man for obtuse quotes is former coach Sepp Herberger. Here are two examples... *'Der Ball ist rund...'* (the ball is round) – meaning that this is the only certainty in the game of football and that really anything can happen. *'Der schnellste Spieler ist der...'* – literal meaning 'the fastest player is the ball'.

- *'Two chances, one goal – that's what I call a 100 per cent chance.'* Roland Wohlfahrt, another German player with a vaguely funny name.

- *'First we had no luck and then bad luck came as well.'* From an interview with ex player Juergen Wegmann.

- *'I had the feeling of a good feeling.'* From an interview with Andreas Möeller who also came up with: *'Milan or Madrid – the most important thing is that it's Italian!'*

- *'Rizitelli and I are a great trio, um, err, quartet.'* Juergen Klinsmann expert diver, German striker and Tottenham star.

- *'Our chances to reach the quarter final are 50:50 or 60:60.'* Reiner Calmund, manager not mathematician, something reinforced by Andreas Brehme who said *'I will only say one word: thank you!'*, proving once again that German players can't do maths.

- Who can forget Franz Beckenbauer, outstanding player and leader, though maths is not his strong point? He once said: *'In one year I played 16 months.'* He was asked by a TV host what the likely outcome of a match was and said: *'Yes, well. There is only one possibility: Victory, tie or defeat!'* Good to see German pundits sit on the fence too.

- *'FC Bavaria is kicked out of the Champions League. These are situations where even Uli Hoeness asks himself, "Hmm…maybe it would be better if the coach was on cocaine."'* Harald Schmidt on the Harald Schmidt Show (yes they gave him TV show), following FC Bavaria Munich's qualifying round elimination from the Champions League in 2002.

- *'In Bremen we didn't want to concede a goal. That worked out well until they scored.'* Thomas Haessler, German player and titchy bloke.

- *'They shouldn't think they are Brazilians just because they come from Brazil.'* Paul Breitner, German player and hairy bloke who also came up with: *'Then came the penalty kick. We were all shitting ourselves, me, I had diarrhoea.'*

- *'At the moment it stands at 1:1. But it could have been the other way around.'* Heribert Fassbender, another funny name, another in need of an abacus. He also came out with this classic where he displayed a talent often seen in Britain – the stating of the bleeding obvious… *'And now the fans chant again: Türkiye, Türkiye. Which means Turkey, Turkey.'* He also demonstrated his knowledge of Germany's neighbours, France: *'Soccer is, in the meantime, number one in France – as is handball.'*

BIG MATCH BINGO

- *'I'm gonna fly somewhere south – maybe Canada or something.'* Mehmet Scholl proving that geography isn't a strong point either.

- Liverpool star Dietmar Hamann shows his language skills are up to speed – he said this as part of his defence when sent off: *'The fact that my opponent knocked me down and hampered my shot at goal I can forget, but when he called me 'Pardon' as well I lost my temper and kicked him.'*

- *'Actually, nobody can beat us. Except ourselves. That's what we are working on.'* Zoltan Sebescen, should do well in the Premiership with logic like this.

- Gyula Lorant shows his observation skills... *'The ball is round. If it had sides, it would be a cube.'*

- Race relations seem to have been an issue, but at least this is a new slant on stereotyping. *'Although the Koreans stink of garlic, it is no reason not to mark them!'* says German businessman Wolfgang Ley, while Marcus Reif shows his powers of observation with: *'You'll recognise the Ghanaians by their yellow socks.'*

- Reporter Jörg Dahlmann did a piece to camera on the farewell for German captain and old boy Lothar Matthaeus... *'There he goes, a great player. A man like Steffi Graf!'*

17

The B****** in the Black

'Because you're Australian and you always beat us at everything…'

Attributed to referee David Elleray when explaining his booking of Aussie footballer Stan Lazarides.

Referee!

The referee's **task** is an **unenviable one**; he takes abuse throughout the match and his decisions are subjected to intense scrutiny. Without the benefit of multiple cameras showing **all angles** or **the luxury of a replay**, the referee is expected to ensure fair play and make sure the players play by the rules.

Players, meanwhile, deny all wrongdoing, put pressure on the ref to get their way and generally try to deceive him or **gain advantage** wherever possible.

It's an **impossible job** and a mystery as to why anyone would want to do it, but we're all glad that some brave souls step forward and take up the challenge.

> *'Then my eyesight started to go and I took up refereeing.'*
>
> Neil Midgley, referee

Let's start with the tackle. It's a skill that some say has largely been lost, that the rules have got stricter and the hard men have disappeared from the game.

☻ There are lots of different types of tackle. From the **innocuous challenge** to the **career-ending shocker**, fouls can be **blatant** or **over the top**, or just a **poor challenge**. The most shocking and the second most reviled thing that happens on a football pitch (the first being spitting at an opponent) is the **two-footed challenge**, especially if **studs are showing**. This is known also as a **cardinal sin**.

⚽ Even if they win the ball the ref must penalise the **tackle from behind**, with the most difficult decisions being made when someone **blocks off the attack**, especially if he's the **last man**.

⚽ Players that admit an offence **hold their hands up to it**.

'I do swear a lot, but the advantage is that having played abroad I can choose a different language from the referee's.'

Jurgen Klinsmann

The referee's knowledge of the rule book, his ability to communicate with the players and his assistants and his powers of observation are always being **called into question**.

⚽ When making a decision the commentator's usual comment is to say that he **adjudged that a foul** or he adjudged it to be a **bookable offence**.

⚽ Over officious refereeing elicits the comment that the ref is **stifling the game** by giving too many free kicks or that he's interested in promoting himself and not the game.

- ⚽ Overzealous assistant referees (linesmen to you and me) are known as **flag happy**. This is especially annoying when a **perfectly good goal** is disallowed.

- ⚽ Commentators (and fans) love it when the game is **allowed to flow** and the referee is good at **playing the advantage**.

> *'What the hell he [the referee] saw I don't know, he ought to go down to Specsavers.'*
>
> **Attributed to Ian Holloway**

When a refereeing decision is made one side is always unhappy about it, which usually results in lots of swearing and players generally **venting their frustration** with lots of **finger pointing**, jabbing and chin jutting.

- ⚽ Small on-field squabbles or **altercations** are classed as **handbags**. More serious fights, usually from an **overreaction**, that result in a sending-off come with the comment that players should know better, especially when **hands are raised**.

- ⚽ Overreactions are best when there's a melee of players all trying to calm each other down, but there's always one player who **runs all of 50 yards to get involved**.

BIG MATCH BINGO

- Players that **show dissent** are always liable **to get penalised** and especially when they overuse **colourful language**. This is usually accompanied by slow-motion clips of the player involved saying 'f**k' and the studio pundits saying 'well we can tell he's unhappy about it'.

- Any bad decision is either **totally unacceptable, out of order** or an **injustice**.

'He was crap!'

**Fulham boss Chris Coleman
on referee Mark Halsey.**

18

Who Said What?

'I don't know much about football. I know what a goal is, which is surely the main thing about football.'

Victoria Beckham

Quotations, Stupid and Wise…

Here is a selection of quotes that I decided to include in the book just because they were too good to leave out… enjoy.

Players on players

- *'I was watching the Blackburn game on TV on Sunday when it flashed on the screen that George (Ndah) had scored in the first minute at Birmingham. My first reaction was to ring him up. Then I remembered he was out there playing.'* – Ade Akinbiyi, slap on head, duh!

- *'If Graeme Souness was a chocolate drop, he'd eat himself.'* – Archie Gemmill, miaow…

- *'The Julie Andrews of football…'* – ex Leeds player Duncan McKenzie on Kevin Keegan.

- *'He's not fit to lace my boots as a player.'* – George Best on Kevin Keegan.

Managers on managers

- *'In England you have a good phrase. It is "to bring the game into disrepute".'* – Arsene Wenger pissed off with Sir Alex Ferguson.

- *'I think he is one of these people who is a voyeur, he likes to watch other people. There are some guys who, when they are at home, have a big telescope to see what happens in other families. He speaks, speaks, speaks about Chelsea.'* – Jose Mourinho losing the plot with Arsene Wenger.

Managers on players

- *'I'm a man of few words, but most of the ones I said to the players began with F.'* – Steve Coppell

- *'England's best centre forward of his type.'* – manager Steve Bruce damning his centre forward Emile Heskey with faint praise.

- *'He's the only man I know who could start an argument with himself.'* – Sir Bobby Robson on Craig Bellamy.

When it just doesn't add up…

- *'I always used to put my right boot on first, and then obviously my right sock.'* – ex Liverpool and Newcastle player Barry Venison on getting dressed.

- *'And Ritchie has now scored 11 goals, exactly double the number he scored last season.'* – Commentator Alan Parry needing one more finger.

WHO SAID WHAT?

Divine intervention

- *'It was not me making those saves, it was God.'* – Brazilian goalkeeper Taffarel, and it could be true given that it's said that Brazilian goalies are generally surplus to requirements.

- *'The Saudis would struggle in Europe because of that problem with those prayers five times a day.'* – ex England coach Don Howe showing his cultural knowledge.

- *'After his first training session in Heaven, George Best, from his favourite right wing, turned the head of God who was filling in at left back. I would love him to save me a place in his team – George Best, that is, not God.'* – Eric Cantona, who else…

- *'God created me to delight people with my goals.'* – Romario, modest little git.

Hold that thought…

- *'If he had won Euro 2004 he could have slept with the guard dog and got away with it.'* – Disgraced politician and football pundit David Mellor on Sven Goran Eriksson.

- *'After you've scored a goal it's just orgasmic… if you asked me just after a game I'd say it's better than sex, but if you asked me just after sex I'd say: "Forget it, mate."'* – Trevor Sinclair confusing his wife or girlfriend.

Sex and football, you have to be worried…

- *'When Manchester United are at their best I am close to orgasm.'* – Gianluca Vialli

- *'I love England, one reason being the magnificent breasts of English girls.'* – Emmanuel Petit

- *'My soccer boots and an inflatable doll, because a month without a woman would be difficult.'* – attributed to Belgian star Eric Deflandre, a lonely boy, when asked what he was taking with him to France.

- *'Right now, everything is going wrong for me – if I fell in a barrel of boobs I'd come out sucking my thumb!'* – Ian Holloway having a tough time of it.

He's Mr Cliché

- *'It's a funny old game but all credit to the Iran lads, they gave 110 per cent.'* – Savo Milosevic

- *'We need to become more ruthless and clinical in front of goal.'* – Gary Neville

- *'The greatest barrier to success is the fear of failure.'* – Sven Goran Eriksson

WHO SAID WHAT?

What the bloody hell are they talking about…?

- *'If Chelsea drop points, the cat's out in the open. And you know what cats are like – sometimes they don't come home.'*
  – Sir Alex Ferguson trying to be clever.

- *'Michael Owen, he's got the legs of a salmon.'* – Craig Brown

- *'There was a spell in the second half when I took my heart off my sleeve and put it in my mouth.'* – QPR manager Ian Holloway

- *'Don't count your eggs until the chicken's laid them.'*
  – Sir Bobby Robson

- *'When the seagulls follow the trawler, it's because they think sardines will be thrown into the sea.'* – Eric Cantona confusing himself and the English media as well.

- *'The unthinkable is not something we are thinking at the moment.'* – Peter Kenyon on another crisis.

Bless 'em

- *'It can be a bit of a hindrance when you walk into a restaurant for a quiet meal and one or two launch into "Psycho, Psycho!"'* – Stuart Pearce on living with that nickname.

- *'I'd like to get ten goals this season, but the authorities don't normally let me play for a whole season.'* – Vinnie Jones in his prime.

- *'All I want is to play regularly.'* – Milan Baros while at Liverpool.

Taste

- *'People say footballers have terrible taste in music but I would dispute that. In the car at the moment I've got The Corrs, Cher, Phil Collins, Shania Twain and Rod Stewart.'* – Sky pundit Andy Gray

Bitch!

- *'Count on Robert Pires to keep his D'Artagnan beard nicely trimmed so he looks formidable as he crumples to the turf just inside the box under a non-existent challenge.'* – The Guardian 2004

- *'*Thunderbirds *puppet who's now made a career out of bleating on and on about Liverpool's injury problems on* Match of the Day.*'* – Zit magazine on Alan Hansen. They also called Messrs Hansen and Lineker Mr & Mrs Mogadon.

- *'Anything that matters so much to David Coleman, you realise doesn't matter much at all.'* – Clive James

19

The Fans

'Even if I am in a bad mood I have to smile and be nice to the fans.

I moisturise daily with Nivea and I regularly use Nivea body lotion.'

Pretty boy, moisturiser user and Arsenal player Freddie Ljungberg

> *'A true football fan is one who knows the nationality of every player in the Republic of Ireland team.'*
>
> **Attributed to musician Ken Bolam**

Supporters, Obsessives and Those who have to Listen to the Bullshit…

We end this book with a tribute to those people who make the **game of football** the worldwide phenomenon that it is – even the USA has a decent team nowadays and football is the number one sport in the majority of countries. It would not be so without the support of the fans.

Fans faithfully follow a crap team, living, breathing and, in their mind, playing every game for the team. **The faithful** take offence easily and hate with a passion those who follow their club only when a big match comes up.

Commentator's hate **so-called fans** when fans are violent (rightly so), but also take the piss (usually gently) when their love for their team leads them to eccentricity. What commentators and pundits are in danger of doing is using clichés and their narrow views to hijack the game from the fans, and this mustn't happen.

Fans make the game what it is today, whether they're dancing in the streets in a small northern town after winning the local derby or getting quietly pissed after yet another demoralising defeat.

Taking their tops off in the middle of winter, singing endlessly even though their team is five-one down, applauding and appreciating real talent when they see it, travelling everywhere to support their team and finding the money to do it, eating all the pies!

For **the neutral** though, or those of us who haven't got the balls to actually support a team (I include myself in this), watching the game provides drama, excitement and the knowledge that someone somewhere is suffering for their team and it's not you.

> *'Nowhere in the world do supporters love their clubs more than in England. England is paradise to play in.'*
>
> Arjen Robben

Sources and acknowledgements

I have tried to get as many confirmed sources as possible through the book using websites, newspaper and magazine archives, books and visual media and to our knowledge the quotes and anecdotes are accurate.

I have named specific sources where I know them, but would like to thank all friends, colleagues and friends of friends who came up with suggestions and sent in stuff.

I'd specifically like to thank Pablo Moreno, Eddy de Rooij, Gaby Kern and Suzanne Muller for their translating skills.

Thanks to Paul Torjussen and Ion Mills at Southbank for kicking me up the backside enough so that I finished the book.

To Michaela for all else that really matters.

'The fans all had the complexion and body scent of a cheese-and-onion crisp and the eyes of pit bulls.'

Writer Martin Amis after watching a football match at QPR.

BULLSHIT BINGO

'Every now and then a book falls into your lap that's so good you feel like punching the air. Bullshit Bingo is one of those books'

The Guardian

Low hanging fruit ....Touch base...Go for it...Bottom Line... Fast Track...Best Practice...Are you swamped by bullshit words and phrases, lies innuendo, boring meetings, two faced colleagues, hopeless managers and a psycho boss?

This book will change your life...!

To order your copy
£6.99 including free postage and packing (UK and Eire only)
£9.99 for overseas orders
For credit card orders phone Turnaround Customer Services on
0208 829 3000 quoting reference 1 904915

For orders via post – cheques payable to Southbank Publishing
21 Great Ormond St, London WC1 3JB
Email to Info@southbankpublishing

WILL WRITE AND DIRECT FOR FOOD
Cartoons by Alan Parker

Sir Alan Parker wrote and directed his first feature film in 1975, *Bugsy Malone*. Fourteen films and three decades later he is preparing his next project. Known for his acidic wit and uncompromising approach to film making, Parker has often resorted to humour in cartoons, to get his view across. This unique collection contains over 200 mini masterpieces from Sir Alan Parker who Will Write and Direct for Food.

To order your copy at a special price
£11.99 including free postage and packing (UK and Eire only)
£14.99 for overseas orders
For credit card orders phone Turnaround Customer Services on
0208 829 3000 quoting reference 1 904915 BMB

For orders via post – cheques payable to Southbank Publishing
21 Great Ormond St, London WC1 3JB
Email to Info@southbankpublishing

THE POWERHOUSE BEHIND LED ZEPPELIN
THE GODFATHER OF ROCK DRUMMING

On 25th September 1980 John Bonham, considered one of the greatest drummers of all time, died in tragic circumstances. Two months later a simple letter signed by Plant, Page and Jones, stated that they could not replace him and therefore could not continue. After nine multi-million selling albums and record breaking world tours, *Led Zeppelin* came to an abrupt and premature end.

With exclusive interviews with band members and contributions from many others that knew him, and including previously un-published photographs from the Bonham collection, this is an important tribute not only to John Bonham but also to Mick Bonham who died soon after completing this book.

To order your copy
£12.99 including free postage and packing (UK and Eire only)
£15.99 for overseas orders
For credit card orders phone Turnaround Customer Services on
0208 829 3000 quoting reference 1 904915

For orders via post – cheques payable to Southbank Publishing
21 Great Ormond St, London WC1 3JB
Email to Info@southbankpublishing

CONFESSIONS OF AN ADVERTISING MAN

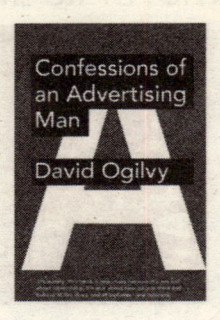

'Ultimately, this book is important because it's not just about advertising, it's also about how people think and behave at the sharp end of business-any business'.

Sir Alan Parker

'Required reading for anyone in the business'
Media Week

'Ogilvy the creative force of modern advertising'
The New York Times

The international best seller is available again from Southbank Publishing. David Ogilvy was an advertising genius and his views are timeless. If you aspire to be a good manager in any kind of business then this is a must read.

To order your copy
£9.99 including free postage and packing (UK and Eire only), £ 12.99 for overseas orders.
For credit card orders phone Turnaround Customers Services on 020 8829 3000 quoting reference 1904915
For orders via post – Cheques payable to Southbank Publishing, 21 Great Ormond St, London, WCI N 3JB, mail to:
Info@southankpublising.com